IPSWICH TOWN
On This Day

IPSWICH TOWN
On This Day

*History, Facts & Figures
from Every Day of the Year*

DAN BOTTEN

IPSWICH TOWN
On This Day

History, Facts & Figures from Every Day of the Year

All statistics, facts and figures are correct as of 31st August 2008

© Dan Botten

Dan Botten has asserted his rights in accordance with the Copyright, Designs and Patents Act 1988 to be identified as the author of this work.

Published By:
Pitch Publishing Ltd,
A2 Yeoman Gate,
Durrington BN13 3QZ

Email: info@pitchpublishing.co.uk
Web: www.pitchpublishing.co.uk

First published 2008

A catalogue record for this book is available from the British Library.

10-digit ISBN: 1-9054112-7-8
13-digit ISBN: 978-1-9054112-7-6
Printed and bound in Great Britain by Cromwell Press

This book is dedicated to
my wife Hilary and son Alex,
for their love, support and patience.

Dan Botten – September 2008

FOREWORD BY SIMON MILTON

My introduction to Ipswich Town Football Club was thanks to Bobby Ferguson, and I can honestly say that I have never looked back from the moment I joined in 1987.

I knew that I was coming into a club that was steeped in history, and that is a great responsibility for any player who pulls on the shirt. When I first arrived the fans would talk to me about legends such as Sir Bobby Robson, Ray Crawford and many others besides.

We went on to create more Town history by winning the Division Two championship in 1992 under John Lyall, and some of the players who played at the club during the 1990s were legends in their own right; and that's not just in Ipswich, but in the game in general.

Now in my 23rd year of working for Ipswich Town on and off the field, I consider myself an adopted Suffolk boy. I thoroughly enjoy my commercial role within the Academy and I am delighted every time a home-grown player makes his debut for the first team.

With Ipswich Town – whether its promotion, relegation or cup runs – there always seems to be something to keep our interest, and I think we are all very lucky to be involved with, and to follow, a club like it.

We all know that the club records are now rich with many marvellous events; a Division One title, Wembley wins, European trophy success – we could go on forever. I know that people will enjoy dipping into a book like this as they try to find some of the moments that may have been special to them.

To all Ipswich Town fans everywhere: you have a great club, and I am proud to be a part of it. Enjoy the read.

Simon Milton, Ipswich Town player 1987-97
Player of The Year 1996, and current academy director

ACKNOWLEDGEMENTS

I'd like to express my gratitude to all those at Pitch Publishing, most notably Dan Tester, for all his enthusiasm, support and advice. Huge thanks must also be made to the following works of reference I have used. *These are The Men Who Made The Town: The Official History of Ipswich Town FC*, from 1878 (John Eastwood and Tony Moyes), *The Who's Who of Ipswich Town* (Dean Hayes), *Ipswich Town, Head to Head* (Peter Waring) and the wonderful www.tmwmtt.com (Ralph Morris). I would also like to thank club archivist, Ian Hunneybell and photographer Owen Hines for their support and finally to Dan Pimm, who has shared many of these wonderful Town experiences alongside me.

INTRODUCTION

Ipswich Town On This Day chronicles the fascinating facts, figures and trivia, for each day of the year, about the club we love: Ipswich Town.

The Blues have enjoyed many amazing highs, and a fair few lows, in their colourful 130-year history. The book starts on January 1st, and follows the action on every date through to December 31st. FA Cup clashes are prominent at the beginning and as we enter April the excitement of promotion run-ins, championships – and relegation battles – intensifies.

May sees FA Cup and Uefa Cup glory and play-off success, and failures. Summer-month activity is more subdued with new faces arriving, old players departing and Town players winning international recognition. August explodes into life as new seasons kick off buoyed by unbridled optimism for what lies ahead… and, after a few months, perhaps pessimism. Incredible matches, amazing scorelines, fantastic, individual feats, unusual goings-on (see if you can find the Portman Road pitch invasion from a horde of rats) and remarkable players all featured throughout.

Many an hour has been spent trawling through old programmes and excellent books by John Eastwood, Tony Moyse, Peter Waring and Dean Hayes to help bring you this account of Ipswich history. It's been a fantastic and educational experience putting it together and I sincerely hope you enjoy reading *Ipswich Town On This Day*, as much as I enjoyed writing it.

Dan Botten – September 2008

IPSWICH TOWN
On This Day

JANUARY

WEDNESDAY 1st JANUARY 1947

Town's first New Year's Day fixture saw them draw 1-1 at Bournemouth & Boscombe Athletic with Camberwell-born Albert Day scoring in front of 8,000 spectators at Dean Court.

TUESDAY 1st JANUARY 1985

Relegation-threatened Town beat neighbours Norwich City 2-0 in the East Anglian derby with 21,710 present fans at Portman Road. Eric Gates settled the hosts before Ipswich-born midfielder Jason Dozzell made it safe in the 65th minute with his first-ever goal against the Canaries.

FRIDAY 1st JANUARY 1988

The Blues picked up their first ever New Year's Day away victory with a 2-1 win at Stoke City. Town's little and large strike partnership struck gold as gangling South African Mich D'Avray and diminutive marksman David Lowe scored in the first half as Town triumphed. A crowd of 9,976 were in attendance at the Victoria Ground.

SATURDAY 2nd JANUARY 1960

The Blues raced to a 5-1 half-time lead on the way to crushing Leyton Orient 6-3 in front of 11,740 fans at Portman Road. Doug Millward, later to successfully manage Baltimore Bays in the NPSL, was the star of the show with a hat-trick. Ray Crawford, Ted Phillips and Jimmy Leadbetter completed the scoring.

MONDAY 2nd JANUARY 1978

Town's miserable away record that season continued with a shot-shy 1-0 defeat at Highbury against The Gunners. Roger Osborne came on as a second half substitute and had little impact. However, that would change five months later when he was brought on against the same opposition at Wembley.

MONDAY 2nd JANUARY 1995

Maldon-born Adam Tanner scored a corking volley on his debut as the Blues beat Leicester City 4-1 in a bottom-of-the-table Premier League clash. Tanner – who later in his career tested positive for cocaine and was subsequently banned for three months by the FA – made 87 Blues appearances and scored 8 goals before joining Peterborough United.

MONDAY 3RD JANUARY 1977

Ipswich's undefeated home record continued as they edged Manchester United at Portman Road and stayed close behind table-toppers Liverpool. A bumper New Year turnout of 30,105 saw Clive Woods notch before an unfortunate own-goal by England's Brian Greenhoff gave Town the points.

SATURDAY 3RD JANUARY 1981

The Blues began that season's FA Cup campaign against Aston Villa; the team who would eventually pip them to the First Division title that season. Paul Mariner's finish was the only goal to earn a tricky tie at Shrewsbury Town.

MONDAY 3RD JANUARY 2005

Former Pilgrim Darren Currie scored twice as Town won 2-1 at Plymouth Argyle. The £250,000 signing from Brighton & Hove Albion scored a controversially-awarded penalty on 67 minutes that incensed the home crowd.

TUESDAY 4TH JANUARY 1949

Michael (Mick) Denis Mills was born in Goldaming, Surrey. Portman Road legend Mills' total of 741 appearances is a club record and during an illustrious career he lifted both the FA and the Uefa Cup. He also won 42 caps for England, captaining them at the 1982 World Cup finals. Mills, who later managed Stoke City and Colchester United, can rightly be considered one of the Ipswich Town greats.

SATURDAY 4TH JANUARY 1964

New York-born Gerard Baker scored a hat-trick as Town walloped Oldham Athletic 6-3 in the FA Cup. Baker was to score 66 goals in 151 Town starts after signing from Hibernian in 1963 for £17,000.

SATURDAY 4TH JANUARY 1997

At a snow-clad City Ground, the Blues were thrashed 3-0 by Stuart Pearce's Nottingham Forest in the FA Cup third round. The game was notable for Ipswich-born future England international Keiron Dyer's debut. The Skilful Dyer made 112 appearances before Newcastle United bought him for £6.5m, the highest fee received for an Ipswich Town player.

SATURDAY 5TH JANUARY 1957

Town's only FA Cup encounter with Fulham ended in a 3-2 reverse. A crowd of 22,199 saw Alf Ramsey's side go down as a late equaliser was ruled out by referee Ken Stokes as time expired prompting a mass protest outside the changing rooms after the final whistle.

SATURDAY 5TH JANUARY 2008

A bizarre decision by referee Mark Halsey to send off Ipswich-born Liam Trotter ruined this FA Cup third round game. England striker David Nugent's winner saw Portsmouth win 1-0.

SATURDAY 6TH JANUARY 1968

Ron Wigg scored twice against Birmingham City as Ipswich stayed close on the heels of their fourth-placed visitors. Dunmow-born Wigg scored 4 times in 5 appearances that season and went on to have notable success at Watford and Rotherham United.

SATURDAY 6TH JANUARY 2001

Town travelled to Conference side Morecambe in the FA Cup third round and avoided a potential upset with a comfortable 3-0 win. Marcus Stewart, Alun Armstrong and Jermaine Wright netted.

SATURDAY 7TH JANUARY 1939

Half-back Jock Hutcheson scored on his debut in a 1-1 FA Cup third round draw at Aston Villa. Two years before, Hutcheson suffered what appeared to be a career-ending injury playing for Chelsea and received compensation from the Football League. They refused his League registration when he signed for Town in June 1938 but he was eligible to play in the FA Cup.

SATURDAY 7TH JANUARY 1961

Town suffered a record FA Cup defeat at Southampton as they went down 7-1 in the third round. Down 6-0 at the break, Town had their revenge by winning Division Two and drawing twice with the Saints that season.

SATURDAY 7TH JANUARY 1978

Ipswich began their FA Cup-winning campaign with a comfortable 2-0 victory at Cardiff City. Mick Mills made a club record 494th appearance, while an excellent display saw forward Paul Mariner strike twice.

SATURDAY 8th JANUARY 1966

Intelligent and combative midfielder Danny Hegan scored the only goal as the Blues defeated Coventry City 1-0. Hegan registered 230 appearances and 38 goals – and also represented the Republic of Ireland – before joining Wolverhampton Wanderers.

SATURDAY 8th JANUARY 1972

Town collected a great point at Elland Road in a 2-2 thriller. It was a day for the Clarke family to remember; Allan scored the equaliser for the hosts after elder brother Frank had opened the scoring for the Blues.

WEDNESDAY 9th JANUARY 1963

Edinburgh-born outside-left Jimmy Leadbetter scored his one and only hat-trick in a 3-2 FA Cup win at Mansfield Town. Known as 'Sticks' due to his wiry build, Leadbetter scored a total of 49 goals in 373 appearances and helped Town win three League titles with his exceptional vision.

SATURDAY 9th JANUARY 1965

David Linighan, a strong and imposing centre back, was born in Hartlepool. Brother to Arsenal's Andy, Linighan made 325 Town appearances after signing from Shrewsbury Town. Skipper when Town won the Division One title in 1992, Linighan also scored 13 goals in an impressive Town career.

SATURDAY 9th JANUARY 1993

Oldham Athletic surprisingly defeated fifth-placed Town 2-1 in front of 15,025 fans, Chris Kiwomya scoring the Blues' goal. Athletic were managed by future Town gaffer Joe Royle and featured ex-Town midfielder Mark Brennan, who scored, and future marksman Ian Marshall.

SATURDAY 10th JANUARY 1948

Aldershot Town were beaten 1-0 in Division Three (South) thanks to a second-half strike from Bill Jennings who finished as top scorer that season with 14 goals.

SATURDAY 10th JANUARY 1953

Despite taking a 2-1 lead at Goodison Park, the Blues went down 3-2 at Everton in the FA Cup third round. A crowd of 42,000 was the highest gate that Ipswich had ever played before.

SATURDAY 10TH JANUARY 1988

The *Match of the Day* cameras were at Portman Road for the first ever 'live' transmission of a home game as Town crashed to a 2-1 defeat to Manchester United in the FA Cup.

MONDAY 11TH JANUARY 1971

Town travelled to St James' Park to face Newcastle United in their first FA Cup meeting. Mitchell put the hosts ahead before Mick Mills struck the equaliser with his first FA Cup goal to take the Geordies back to Portman Road. Town would win the replay 2-1.

SATURDAY 11TH JANUARY 2003

Ipswich stretched an unbeaten run to eight games but only had themselves to blame for failing to win at Turf Moor. Spaniard Pablo Counago put Town ahead before going off after a clash of heads with future Blue Drissa Diallo.

SATURDAY 12TH JANUARY 1952

Goalkeeper Mick Burns became the oldest player to represent the Blues in a first-team fixture against Gateshead which ended 2-2 in the FA Cup third round. Burns was 43-years-old.

SATURDAY 12TH JANUARY 1991

Striker Steve Whitton, signed by John Lyall from Sheffield Wednesday for £150,000, scored on his debut as Town beat West Bromwich Albion. He struggled with injuries at Portman Road, but was a regular in midfield during the 1991-92 promotion-winning side. Whitton joined Colchester United, who he later managed, having scored 19 goals for Town.

MONDAY 13TH JANUARY 1969

Bobby Robson was appointed Ipswich's sixth manager. The former England striker had been sacked by Fulham a year earlier after only 18 months in his first management job. He won the post after meeting director Murray Sangster while scouting at Portman Road for Chelsea.

SATURDAY 13TH JANUARY 1981

Town moved to the top spot in English football with a five-goal thrashing of struggling Birmingham City. The goals were shared between Terry Butcher, John Wark, Paul Mariner, Arnold Muhren and Alan Brazil.

MONDAY 13TH JANUARY 1986

Due to the tragic Bradford City fire eight months earlier, Town's 1-0 victory in this FA Cup fixture was witnessed by 10,208 fans at Elland Road. Mark Brennan struck the winner in extra time: it was the first of three Blues games that season to go into an extra 30 minutes.

SATURDAY 14TH JANUARY 1961

Inspirational right-winger Roy Stephenson, renowned for his creative wing-play, scored twice as Bristol Rovers were seen off 3-2 at Portman Road as Ipswich marched towards the Second Division title.

SATURDAY 14TH JANUARY 1989

On a freezing day, Town travelled to rock-bottom Walsall at Fellows Park and crushed the hosts 4-2. John Wark, Jason Dozzell, Chris Kiwomya and Iain Redford scored for John Duncan's men.

SATURDAY 14TH JANUARY 1995

In one of the great Premiership shocks, doomed Ipswich won 1-0 at Anfield to register their first victory in Liverpool at the 34th attempt. Adam Tanner scored the first-half goal: a bright spot in an otherwise miserable season.

TUESDAY 15TH JANUARY 1884

The London Pilgrims visited Ipswich Association to play a benefit match for the East Suffolk Hospital. It was the first time Ipswich Association had played at Portman Road and the permission of the rugby club had to be found. The score and crowd were not recorded.

MONDAY 15TH JANUARY 1979

Sandwiched between two Portman Road victories against Carlisle United and Wolverhampton Wanderers, Town jetted over to Dubai to play Al Ahli to mark the opening of the Red Knights' new stadium. Town won 3-0.

SATURDAY 15TH JANUARY 2000

Ipswich beat bottom club Swindon Town 3-0. The game was memorable for the fine reception afforded Blues full-back Gary Croft who played wearing an electronic tag after returning to action after admitting to a string of motoring offences. At the time, the Robins were in dire financial straits and reported to be losing £25,000 a week.

WEDNESDAY 16TH JANUARY 1952

After a draw four days earlier, Town travelled up to Gateshead in an FA Cup relay which ended 3-3 after extra time. Striker Peter Dobson scored a brace and Stirling-born winger Jimmy Roberts grabbed the other goal. The second replay was staged at Bramall Lane and saw Ipswich's cup campaign end in a 2-1 defeat.

SATURDAY 16TH JANUARY 1954

The Blues stayed seven points clear at the top of Division Three (South) with a 2-1 triumph at Leyton Orient. Tommy Parker and John Elsworthy's goals meant Town had scored in 33 consecutive games.

SATURDAY 17TH JANUARY 1999

Jim Magilton made his Ipswich debut in a 2-1 defeat at table-toppers Sunderland. Matt Holland's wonder goal was not enough despite Mackem supremo Peter Reid lauding the Blues for putting on a "hell of a performance".

SATURDAY 17TH JANUARY 2004

Town's Jekyll and Hyde season continued with a ten-goal thriller, as the Championship's then-top-scoring side beat struggling Crewe Alexandra 6-4 at Portman Road. Tommy Miller and Shefki Kuqi scored twice while half of Crewe's tally came from own goals by Matt Richards and John McGreal. Pablo Counago and Martijn Reuser sealed a breathless affair.

SATURDAY 18TH JANUARY 1936

Born in Liverpool, defender Larry Carberry was spotted by Alf Ramsey playing for The King's Regiment against Bury Town. Carberry made an immediate impression in Suffolk due to his pace and superb timing; he was one of five players to win Championship medals in all three divisions with Ipswich. He didn't score in his 283 appearances.

SATURDAY 18TH JANUARY 1969

Bobby Robson's first game in charge of Ipswich Town saw them travel to Everton and face their third-placed hosts in front of 41,725 fans. In his final season, Ray Crawford scored twice while Joe Royle played up front for the Toffees in the 2-2 draw.

SATURDAY 19TH JANUARY 2002

Ipswich's Town five-match winning Premiership run continued with a 3-1 victory at Derby County which lifted the Blues out of the relegation zone. Majestic finishes from Marcus Bent, Sixto Peralta and Martijn Reuser sealed a memorable win.

SATURDAY 20TH JANUARY 1973

The Blues won only their second game at White Hart Lane with a 1-0 victory over Tottenham Hotspur. Bryan Hamilton's second-half goal took Ipswich Town up to fourth in Division One. A ticket that day in the East Stand cost just 90p.

SATURDAY 20TH JANUARY 2001

Striker Marcus Stewart scored for the seventh successive game as the Tractor Boys took the lead at Stamford Bridge before crashing 4-1 at Chelsea.

SATURDAY 21ST JANUARY 1956

Tom Garneys scored a hat-trick as table-topping Ipswich thrashed Northampton Town 5-0 in front of 13,103 fans. Welsh international Billy Reed and Tommy Parker were the other scorers.

SATURDAY 21TH JANUARY 1989

Stoke City were thumped 5-1 at Portman Road as Sergei Baltacha, the first ever Soviet to play in English football, scored on his debut. The USSR sweeper, who won 46 caps for his country, was signed from Dynamo Kiev but failed to settle at Town due to constantly being played out of position. He left for St Johnstone after 30 appearances and his daughter Elena represented Great Britain at Wimbledon in .

SATURDAY 22ND JANUARY 1966

A poor performance at Division Four Southport saw Ipswich draw 0-0 in the FA Cup third round. Southport dumped Bill McGarry's men out of the competition three days later in a shock 3-2 victory at Haig Avenue.

TUESDAY 22ND JANUARY 1991

The Blues' only win on this day came at Portman Road as they pipped Oxford United 2-1 in a Full Members Cup third round affair. Simon Milton and Jason Dozzell sunk the Us.

WEDNESDAY 23rd JANUARY 1952

Dutchman Frans Thijssen was one of Ipswich Town's greatest signings. Costing £200,000 from FC Twente, the midfield maestro's immaculate control and skill was in abundance in the 1980/81 campaign when he was named the Football Writers' Association Footballer of the Year. He appeared 14 times for his country, scoring three goals, and also scored in both legs of the Uefa Cup Final win against AZ Alkmaar.

SATURDAY 23rd JANUARY 1971

Centre-half Billy Baxter made his 459th and final Blues start in a 1-1 draw with West Bromwich Albion in the FA Cup fourth round.

SATURDAY 23rd JANUARY 1982

Town conquered Luton Town 3-0 in an FA Cup fourth round game at Kenilworth Road. Physical centre-back Terry Butcher's horrific nose injury required 15 pints of blood at a post-match transfusion.

TUESDAY 23rd JANUARY 1996

Popular Canadian right-back Frank Yallop made his final appearance in an Ipswich shirt in a 4-2 Anglo-Italian Cup defeat against Port Vale. He scored 8 goals in 385 games before joining Tampa Bay Mutiny. Yallop, who collected 52 caps for Canada while with Town, was to eventually manage his national team before signing David Beckham to LA Galaxy.

SATURDAY 24th JANUARY 1959

Derek Rees struck as the Blues won 1-0 at Stoke City in the FA Cup fourth round in their first ever triumph over the Potters. Welsh inside-forward Rees scored 32 goals in 95 games before leaving for Welling Town.

SATURDAY 24th JANUARY 1976

Ipswich rarely troubled future custodian Phil Parkes in a 0-0 FA Cup fourth round game with Wolverhampton Wanderers.

WEDNESDAY 25th JANUARY 1928

Welsh wizard Billy Reed has the distinction of being Town's first player to be capped at international level. Born in Rhondda, his exceptional dribbling prowess saw him christened the 'Stanley Matthews' of the Third Division. He scored 46 times in 169 starts for the Blues before joining Swansea City.

SATURDAY 25th JANUARY 1958

Two goals from Bobby Charlton saw Manchester United beat Ipswich 2-0 in an FA Cup fourth round tie watched by 53,550 fans. Sadly, it was the last time that the great 'Busby Babes' were to play at Old Trafford as the Munich air disaster happened less than two weeks later.

SATURDAY 25th JANUARY 1975

Mick Mills scored the only goal as Liverpool were seen off 1-0 in the FA Cup. A record Portman Road attendance for the competition, 34,709, watched Town's only domestic cup victory over the Reds to date.

SATURDAY 26th JANUARY 1957

Ted Phillips slammed a hat-trick as Ipswich slaughtered Shrewsbury Town 5-1 and kept up their march towards finishing top of Division Three (South). That season, Phillips was to finish with 41 league goals and five hat-tricks thanks to his fierce shooting.

SATURDAY 26th JANUARY 1980

Paul Mariner's winner in a 2-1 FA Cup fourth round win at Bristol City was his sixth goal in five games.

SATURDAY 26th JANUARY 1985

Electric Northern Ireland striker Kevin 'Jockey' Wilson poached a goal on his debut as Town defeated Gillingham 3-2 at Portman Road. Wilson cost the Blues £150,000 from Derby County at a time when funds were short due to the building of the Pioneer Stand. He was later signed by Chelsea and banked the club a £175,000 profit after notching 49 goals in 125 games.

WEDNESDAY 27th JANUARY 1937

Ipswich went top of the Southern League with a 2-1 victory at Aldershot Town reserves. The crowd of 975 is the smallest to witness a Town league game on their travels since turning professional.

SATURDAY 27th JANUARY 1979

Over forty league and FA Cup matches were postponed due to Arctic conditions but the Blues' 0-0 FA Cup fourth round clash with Leyton Orient went ahead after flamethrowers cleared ice from oe of the Portman Road goalmouths.

MONDAY 28TH JANUARY 1963

Ipswich announced that their new manager to replace Alf Ramsey would be 38-year-old Jackie Milburn who was player/coach of Southern League Yiewsley. The former Newcastle United forward had won 13 England caps in a glittering playing career.

SATURDAY 28TH JANUARY 1978

Town eventually cruised into the FA Cup fifth round with a 4-1 drubbing of plucky Fourth Division Hartlepool United who, at the time, were 91st in the Football League. South African Colin Viljoen scored twice in his final season with the club while Paul Mariner's volley was his third goal of the cup campaign. England international Brian Talbot clinched the victory with a stylish winner.

MONDAY 28TH JANUARY 1985

An explosive, highly-charged encounter saw the Blues win 2-1 at Queens Park Rangers in a League Cup fifth round replay. Russell Osman and Simon Stainrod were sent off for fighting as Ipswich fans came under a barrage of missiles from disgruntled home fans.

SATURDAY 29TH JANUARY 1977

A 2-2 draw with Wolverhampton Wanderers in the FA Cup was watched by 32,996 in Suffolk. Right-back George Burley and Paul Mariner netted.

SATURDAY 29TH JANUARY 1994

Tottenham Hotspur were thumped 3-0 at Portman Road in the FA Cup as goals from Neil Thompson, Gavin Johnson and Ian Marshall swept them aside. Sol Campbell replaced ex-Town midfielder Jason Dozzell late on.

SATURDAY 30TH JANUARY 1954

The Blues won their first ever FA Cup fourth round tie with a goal from Billy Reed. Birmingham City, including England goalkeeper Gil Merrick, were beaten 1-0.

SATURDAY 30TH JANUARY 1965

Before Ipswich's 5-0 FA Cup thrashing at Tottenham Hotspur there was a minute's silence for Sir Winston Churchill who had died a few days earlier. Jimmy Greaves scored a hat-trick for the Londoners.

SATURDAY 30TH JANUARY 1982

A shock 3-1 Portman Road defeat to Notts County snapped a run of nine straight wins for Town as they stayed third in Division One.

SATURDAY 31ST JANUARY 1970

The Blues fought back at Hillsborough to pick up a precious point against Sheffield Wednesday. Mick Mills and striker Mick Hill scored late on in a four-goal thriller to shock a crowd of 17,630.

SATURDAY 31ST JANUARY 1998

Substitute Alex Mathie scored two late goals as Bradford City were beaten 2-1 in Suffolk. The Bantams had ex-Ipswich centre-back Eddie Youds sent off for two bookable offences.

IPSWICH TOWN
On This Day

FEBRUARY

WEDNESDAY 1st FEBRUARY 1939

Prolific forward Fred Chadwick's goal saw off Northampton Town 1-0 in a Southern Section Cup first round replay. The crowd of 2,858 is the lowest ever at Portman Road in a competitive match.

SUNDAY 1st FEBRUARY 1953

Following a 4-1 stuffing at Torquay United, and a long journey home, the Town players found themselves marooned at Ipswich station for five hours due to extensive flooding along the east coast.

SATURDAY 1st FEBRUARY 1969

Bobby Robson's first game at Portman Road as manager saw his troops defeat Manchester United, including George Best, 1-0 at Portman Road in front of a then-record crowd of 30,837.

SATURDAY 2nd FEBRUARY 1974

Two goals apiece from Bryan Hamilton and Trevor Whymark inspired Ipswich to a 7-0 Division One romp over Southampton at Portman Road.

TUESDAY 2nd FEBRUARY 1982

Town were playing in the League Cup semi-finals for the first time but a poor display saw them lose 2-0 to Liverpool at Portman Road in the first leg.

SATURDAY 3rd FEBRUARY 1968

In one of the most exciting local derbies ever, the Blues squeaked past Norwich City 4-3 at Carrow Road before 30,000 fans. Colin Viljoen's hat-trick in 26 minutes turned round a 2-0 deficit after 30 minutes.

SATURDAY 4th FEBRUARY 1950

A 1-0 win over fellow strugglers Exeter City moved Town off the bottom of Division Three (South) thanks to a strike from John Gibbons.

SATURDAY 4th FEBRUARY 1984

Aged 16 years and 56 days, Jason 'Dozy' Dozzell became the youngest player to appear in a league match for the Blues. He scored on his debut in a 3-1 victory against Coventry City and was to eventually leave for Tottenham Hotspur in a £1.9m deal after notching 73 strikes in 416 games.

SATURDAY 5TH FEBRUARY 1983

The brand new Pioneer Stand was opened and Ipswich marked the day by drawing 1-1 with Manchester United. The stand cost £1.4m to build and had a capacity for 4,800 seated spectators. Sir Stanley Rous was present at the unveiling.

SATURDAY 5TH FEBRUARY 2000

Bristolian Marcus Stewart, signed from Huddersfield Town for £2.5m, scored on his debut as Barnsley were beaten 2-0 at Oakwell.

SATURDAY 6TH FEBRUARY 1904

Town travelled to Colchester Town and recorded a 4-2 victory to take them above Harwich and Parkeston to win their first ever league championship. Goals from Maldon (2), Mills and Phillips clinched the South East Anglian League.

MONDAY 6TH FEBRUARY 1984

Rapid striker Darren Bent was born in Tooting. The youngster was purchased by Charlton Athletic in the summer of 2005 for £2.5m, after grabbing 55 goals in 115 Town starts. He went on to play for England and after Charlton's relegation from the Premiership in 2007 he joined Spurs for a fee of £16m.

SATURDAY 7TH FEBRUARY 1981

A 3-2 win over Crystal Palace before 25,036 fans saw Ipswich stay top of Division One on goal difference. Paul Mariner scored at both ends before another own-goal, this time from Palace's Billy Gilbert, saw Town take the victory.

SATURDAY 8TH FEBRUARY 1975

Liverpool crushed the Blues 5-2 at Anfield in Division One. At the final whistle just five points separated the top flight's top eleven teams.

SATURDAY 8TH FEBRUARY 1992

Ipswich's excellent season continued as they destroyed fellow promotion chasers Portsmouth 5-2 at Portman Road. The win saw Town move into second place in Division Two. Jason Dozzell and Chris Kiwomya grabbed a brace apiece.

SATURDAY 9TH FEBRUARY 1980

Town achieved only their second win in seventeen attempts at Goodison Park with a fabulous 4-0 triumph. Brazil (2), Gates and Mariner scored the goals as Ipswich stretched their unbeaten run to twelve games.

SATURDAY 9TH FEBRUARY 2002

Town were brought crashing down to earth following four consecutive Premiership victories with a record 6-0 home defeat by Liverpool.

SATURDAY 10TH FEBRUARY 1962

The Blues shook up the race for the Division One title with a 2-1 victory at Fulham thanks to a Ray Crawford winner. It was their first win over the Cottagers in eight attempts.

SATURDAY 10TH FEBRUARY 1968

Bill McGarry's champions-elect slipped to a surprise 4-1 defeat at Carlisle United. South African Colin Viljoen scored and was then later substituted.

MONDAY 11TH FEBRUARY 1963

Hard-working midfielder Glenn Pennyfather was born in Billericay. Blond-haired Pennyfather was a squad member in the 1991/92 Second Division title campaign.

SATURDAY 11TH FEBRUARY 2006

Matt Richards' late penalty ensured Ipswich beat Burnley 2-1. Richards became the youngest player to represent the club in European competition when appearing in the Uefa Cup in 2002 against Avenir Beggen.

MONDAY 12TH FEBRUARY 1923

Doug Rees, who owns the dubious honour of scoring seven own goals, the most ever by a Town player, was born in Neath. Rees made 386 starts before retiring.

SATURDAY 12TH FEBRUARY 2000

Marcus Stewart scored on his home debut against his previous owners Huddersfield Town who were seen off 2-1. The Blues moved to third in Division One.

WEDNESDAY 13TH FEBRUARY 1924

Tommy Parker, who made 475 Ipswich appearances as a wing half/inside-forward was born in Hartlepool. Parker – an English schoolboy rugby international and keen fishermen – scored 95 goals and was Alf Ramsey's first captain at Portman Road. Parker stayed with the club in various capacities for 20 years after he hung up his boots.

SATURDAY 13TH FEBRUARY 1937

Scottish international Bobby Bruce scored twice at Cheltenham Town in a 3-1 Southern League victory. Bruce went on to net seven goals in five games.

SATURDAY 13TH FEBRUARY 1993

Grimsby Town were blown away 4-0 at Portman Road in an FA Cup fifth round tie as Bulgarian marksman Bontcho Guentchev scored Town's only hat-trick in the competition in the last 24 years (up to December 2008).

SATURDAY 14TH FEBRUARY 1953

The Blues administered their own Valentine's Day massacre at the Goldstone Ground as Brighton & Hove Albion were despatched 4-1. It was Ipswich's first win at The Seagulls in eight attempts.

SATURDAY 14TH FEBRUARY 1998

Huddersfield Town were taken apart 5-1 at Portman Road with Jamaican livewire David Johnson (2), Matt Holland, Alex Mathie and Richard Naylor netting.

SATURDAY 15TH FEBRUARY 1975

Northern Ireland midfielder Bryan Hamilton's brace enabled Town to beat Aston Villa 3-2 in the FA Cup fifth round at Portman Road.

TUESDAY 15TH FEBRUARY 1977

Trevor Whymark's scintillating hat-trick saw Norwich City destroyed 5-0 at Portman Road as the Blues leapt to Division One's summit. John Wark and Paul Mariner grabbed the other two goals.

SATURDAY 16TH FEBRUARY 1924

The first Ipswich programme was on show at Portman Road as Town defeated Old Parkonians 2-0 in the Southern Amateur League.

TUESDAY 16TH FEBRUARY 1960

Town celebrated the turning on of their newly-installed £15,000 floodlights with a 4-0 friendly drubbing of Arsenal.

TUESDAY 16TH FEBRUARY 1982

Blues crushed First Division leaders Southampton 5-2 at Portman Road. Alan Brazil hit five, including three in five minutes. Kevin Keegan scored for the Saints.

SATURDAY 17TH FEBRUARY 1973

A Bryan Hamilton brace moved Ipswich third in Division One with a 4-1 home win over Manchester United in front of a record crowd – 31,857.

SATURDAY 17TH FEBRUARY 2007

The Tractor Boys gallantly went down at Premiership Watford in the FA Cup fifth round. Damien Francis scored the only goal as an under-strength Town battered their hosts into submission despite seeing debut-making Irishman George O'Callaghan sent off.

TUESDAY 18TH FEBRUARY 1969

The Blues achieved a brilliant 2-0 win at Highbury over fourth-placed Arsenal thanks to goals from Ray Crawford and John O'Rourke.

SATURDAY 18TH FEBRUARY 1978

In freezing conditions at Bristol Rovers, Ipswich kept their name in the FA Cup quarter-final draw thanks to a brace from reserve striker Robin Turner. Turner's goals, including a leveller four minutes from time, were his first for the club. Winger Clive Woods was the Town man of the match with a performance which made the hosts defence look as 'petrified as Laurel and Hardy swinging on loose scaffolding.'

SATURDAY 19TH FEBRUARY 1972

The Blues were sunk by a solitary Charlie George goal at Portman Road before a crowd of 28,657 fans.

WEDNESDAY 19TH FEBRUARY 1986

Dean McDonald was born in Lambeth. McDonald scored his only goal at Crewe Alexandra before joining Gillingham on a free after five starts.

SATURDAY 20TH FEBRUARY 1954

Town slumped to a 6-1 defeat in their first-ever FA Cup fifth round tie at First Division Preston North End. The Lillywhites, boasting Tom Finney and Tommy Docherty, romped home in front of 34,500 fans and were to eventually lose 3-2 to West Bromwich Albion in the Wembley final.

SATURDAY 20TH FEBRUARY 1982

Leeds United were brushed aside 2-0 at Elland Road as goals from Mick Mills and Alan Brazil sent the Blues fifth in Division One.

FRIDAY 21ST FEBRUARY 1992

Midfielder Simon Milton's vital long-ranger saw off Tranmere Rovers 1-0 and kept Ipswich second in Division Two.

SATURDAY 21ST FEBRUARY 1998

A first-half hat-trick from Scotsman Alex Mathie saw the Blues batter Norwich City in a 5-0 drubbing at Portman Road. Dutch winger Bobby Petta also scored a classy brace.

TUESDAY 22ND FEBRUARY 1994

A snowy Portman Road witnessed an exciting Premier League clash as Sheffield United lost 3-2 thanks to a wonder goal from stylish winger Stuart Slater.

SATURDAY 22ND FEBRUARY 1975

Alun Armstrong was born in Gateshead. The £500,000 signing's undoubted highlight at Portman Road was scoring in both legs of the Uefa Cup third round ties against Inter Milan.

THURSDAY 23RD FEBRUARY 1922

Welsh winger Ken Wookey was born in Newport. He played 15 times in the 1950/51 Division Three (South) campaign.

SATURDAY 23RD FEBRUARY 1957

only
makes 4
goals!

Doug Millward scored Ipswich's fastest ever goal after only 10 seconds in a 5-0 drubbing of Newport County in Division Three (South) . Ted Phillips, Neil Myles and another for Millward completed the scoring.

SATURDAY 24TH FEBRUARY 1968

John O'Rourke, signed by Bobby Robson weeks earlier, scored twice on his Town debut as Cardiff City were beaten 4-2 at Portman Road.

TUESDAY 24TH FEBRUARY 1998

Stocky speedster David Johnson netted his first career hat-trick against Oxford United as the Blues set a new club record by scoring five goals in their third successive home game in a 5-2 victory.

SATURDAY 25TH FEBRUARY 1978

A vital 1-0 victory at Newcastle United – courtesy of Clive Woods' goal – saw Ipswich win a vital Division One relegation clash.

SATURDAY 25TH FEBRUARY 1995

Goal machine Alex Mathie marked his debut with a goal as Southampton were seen off 2-1 at Portman Road. It was the last time the Blues were to trouble the scorers for seven consecutive games.

MONDAY 26TH FEBRUARY 1979

Holders Ipswich smashed Bristol Rovers 6-1 in the FA Cup fifth round. Alan Brazil scored twice as Town raced to a 4-0 half-time lead.

WEDNESDAY 26TH FEBRUARY 1992

The Blues fell to wonder goals from Jan Molby and Steve McManaman in extra-time as Liverpool were pushed all the way in an FA Cup fifth round tie. The Sky cameras captured a stunning Ipswich performance which included a glorious header from Gavin Johnson to put them 2-1 up.

SATURDAY 27TH FEBRUARY 1937

Town stayed top of the Southern League with a 3-2 victory over Bath City in the West Country. On a heavily waterlogged pitch, goals from George McLuckie, Bobby Bruce and Jock Carter were watched by Swindon Town's squad whose game was postponed.

MONDAY 27TH FEBRUARY 1939

A paltry crowd of just 300, the lowest ever crowd to watch an Ipswich competitive fixture since turning professional, saw Port Vale beat Town 2-0 in a Southern Section Cup second round encounter.

TUESDAY 28TH FEBRUARY 1978

The Blues marched through to the FA Cup quarter-finals overcoming a resilient Bristol Rovers 3-0 at Portman Road in front of 29,090 fans at Portman Road. Skipper Mick Mills' early strike fired dreams of a Wembley day out for the Ipswich faithful. Paul Mariner's header and a 25-yard wonder strike from Clive Woods booked an infamous trip to Millwall in the last eight of the competition.

SATURDAY 28TH FEBRUARY 1981

Town extended their 15-game unbeaten run by running amok at Highfield Road in a 4-0 victory. Finishes from Russell Osman, Eric Gates, Steve McCall and Alan Brazil kept the Blues top of Division One.

TUESDAY 29TH FEBRUARY 1972

Swedish international striker Niklas Gudmundsson was born. He spent two months on loan at Portman Road from Blackburn Rovers at the end of the 1996/97 season and scored three important goals in 10 games.

SATURDAY 29TH FEBRUARY 1992

An important 2-0 home win over Plymouth Argyle kept Ipswich behind leaders Blackburn Rovers in Division Two. Chris Kiwomya and Steve Whitton scored in the second half.

IPSWICH TOWN
On This Day

MARCH

SATURDAY 1st MARCH 1980

Paul Mariner scored a hat-trick as Town walloped second-placed Manchester United 6-0 at Portman Road. United keeper Gary Bailey was his team's hero as he also saved three penalties.

SATURDAY 1st MARCH 2008

All-action midfielder David Norris – signed from Plymouth Argyle for £2m – scored a fine goal in a 1-1 draw at Southampton in the Championship.

SUNDAY 2nd MARCH 1986

Bobby Ferguson took his troops away from the cold winter weather back home with a questionable 15-hour trip to Baghdad to play an Iraq National XI. Trevor Putney's strike on 60 minutes won the game for Ipswich in front of just 3,000 fans.

TUESDAY 3rd MARCH 1964

Jackie Milburn's Town lost 3-2 at Lowestoft Town in a friendly which witnessed the official turning on of the floodlights at Crown Meadow.

SATURDAY 3rd MARCH 1956

A Wilf Grant hat-trick inspired the Blues to a 5-0 pasting of Millwall at The Den in Division Three (South).

WEDNESDAY 4th MARCH 1981

On one of the great European nights, Ipswich demolished St Etienne 4-1 at the Geoffry-Guichard stadium in front of 40,000 expectant Frenchmen in the Uefa Cup quarter-final, first leg. Les Verts, boasting Michel Platini in their ranks, were picked apart despite scoring first through Dutchman Johnny Rep's header. Withstanding heavy early pressure, Paul Mariner's bullet header at the back post levelled the scores. Arnold Muhren's fierce 25-yarder edged the Blues ahead four minutes later and subsequent swift counter attacks saw Mariner score his second before John Wark headed home his 30th goal of the season and 11th in the competition.

SATURDAY 4th MARCH 1995

From the sublime to the ridiculous. Andy Cole scored five times as Ipswich suffered their joint worst away defeat – and Manchester United their biggest win for a century – in a 9-0 Premiership whitewash at Old Trafford.

SATURDAY 5TH MARCH 1949

Bill Jennings scored twice as Ipswich beat Northampton Town 4-2 in a Division Three (South) encounter. Jennings, the son of a Norwich City player, netted 23 goals in 37 outings that season.

SATURDAY 5TH MARCH 1977

Bobby Robson's men won 4-1 at Arsenal in Division One thanks to goals from Brian Talbot, John Wark, Keith Bertschin and Paul Mariner.

SATURDAY 6TH MARCH 1976

Stocky goalkeeper Laurie Sivell suffered a bad facial injury when diving at the feet of future Sky Sports pundit Andy Gray in the 89th minute. The Blues picked up a 0-0 draw after Trevor Whymark replaced Sivell.

TUESDAY 6TH MARCH 2007

Ipswich achieved their first away win in thirteen attempts, and first away goal in seven games, by thumping Hull City 5-2 at the KC Stadium. The goals were shared between Francis Jeffers, Jaime Peters, Alan Lee, Jason De Vos and Danny Haynes.

TUESDAY 7TH MARCH 1961

On a bleak evening, Town turned in a magnificent performance to beat Sheffield United 3-1 at Bramall Lane – packed with 35,057 fans – to march to the top of the Second Division.

SATURDAY 7TH MARCH 1981

The Blues' new £65,000 Volvo executive coach was vandalised during a creditable 3-3 draw at the City Ground against Nottingham Forest in the FA Cup quarter-final.

SATURDAY 8TH MARCH 1975

A record Portman Road crowd of 38,010 saw Ipswich and Leeds United slug out a drab goalless draw in the FA Cup quarter-final. The Portman Stand extensions were in use for the first time.

WEDNESDAY 8TH MARCH 1995

Liverpool-born defender Eddie Youds played his 59th and final Town game in a 3-0 thrashing at Tottenham Hotspur in the Premiership.

THURSDAY 9TH MARCH 1950

Roger Osborne, the Blues' FA Cup-winning goalscorer in 1978, was born in Otley. During his eight seasons at Ipswich he showed his versatility by usually being asked to mark the opposition's most dangerous player. He joined Colchester United after 148 outings.

SATURDAY 9TH MARCH 1963

Keeper Wilf Hall was carried off after ten minutes in a 6-1 thrashing at West Bromwich Albion. Striker Ted Phillips took over in goal as Town were down to nine men for the last 25 minutes after Doug Moran suffered an injury.

SATURDAY 10TH MARCH 1956

Jimmy Leadbetter scored the first of his 49 Ipswich goals in a 3-3 draw at home to Reading. The Edinburgh-born left-winger was signed by Alf Ramsey and is one of a handful of players to win championship medals in three divisions with the same club.

SATURDAY 10TH MARCH 2001

Right-back Chris Makin made his Blues debut in a 2-1 defeat at Aston Villa. Signed from Sunderland for £1.4m, Makin made over 90 appearances in three years.

SATURDAY 11TH MARCH 1978

A sublime performance saw tempestuous hosts Millwall smashed 6-1 at Cold Blow Lane and Ipswich reach the FA Cup semi-finals for the second time in their history. The performance was overshadowed by scenes off the pitch as referee Bill Gow had to order the players off for 20 minutes after George Burley's long-range cracker. Running battles on the terraces between Millwall fans and the police saw a number of spectators spill on to the pitch and individual Town fans attacked in an intimidating atmosphere. When play finally resumed a Paul Mariner hat-trick and goals from John Wark and Brian Talbot made it a day Town fans wouldn't forget for varying reasons.

WEDNESDAY 11TH MARCH 1987

Crestfallen Ipswich missed out on a Wembley appearance as they lost 3-0 at Blackburn Rovers in the now defunct Full Members' Cup semi-final.

SATURDAY 12TH MARCH 1887

The Blues won their first-ever trophy when Ipswich Association beat Ipswich School 2-1 in the Suffolk Challenge Cup Final at Portman Road. In snowy conditions, Sherrington and Peecock scored the goals in front of 1,000 fans.

SATURDAY 12TH MARCH 2005

Nottingham Forest were demolished 6-0 in Suffolk as the Tractor Boys recorded their biggest victory under Joe Royle. Five different players got on the score sheet.

SATURDAY 13TH MARCH 1937

Inside-forward Jock Sowerby played for England in a 1-0 defeat to Scotland at Dulwich. He was described as 'the best forward on show' in front of a 16,000 crowd.

SATURDAY 13TH MARCH 1993

A seven-goal thriller saw Ipswich go down at The Dell despite goals from David Linighan, Paul Goddard and Chris Kiwomya. Ex-England striker Goddard's strike was his last for Ipswich before joining the coaching staff.

WEDNESDAY 14TH MARCH 1962

A packed White Hart Lane saw Alf Ramsey's side continue their march to the Division One title with a 3-1 victory in their first game at Spurs. Dynamic partnership Ray Crawford and Ted Phillips (2) scored the goals.

SATURDAY 14TH MARCH 1959

Clive Baker was born in North Walsham, Norfolk. Baker, an agile and consistent keeper, was the first Town stopper to keep a clean sheet at Liverpool before knee injuries forced him to retire after 58 games.

SATURDAY 15TH MARCH 1975

A pulsating Division One clash saw the Blues defeat visitors Newcastle United 5-4. Bryan Hamilton's hat-trick kept Bobby Robson's boys on course for a third-placed finish.

SATURDAY 15TH MARCH 2003

Captain fantastic Matt Holland scored an early goal in a 1-0 win at Sheffield Wednesday which cemented Ipswich's Division One play-off credentials.

WEDNESDAY 16TH MARCH 1977

Town crashed 4-0 at West Bromwich Albion who were inspired by a Bryan Robson hat-trick. Laurie Sivell, groggy after being kicked in the head by Baggies striker Dave Cross, conceded every goal in the last 20 minutes.

TUESDAY 16TH MARCH 2004

Darren Bent scored his one and only hat-trick for promotion-chasing Town as Walsall were beaten 3-1 at the Bescot Stadium.

SATURDAY 17TH MARCH 1956

A 2-0 win at Watford kept the Blues breathing hard down leaders Leyton Orient's necks in Division Three (South).

SATURDAY 17TH MARCH 2001

The Blues won their first game at West Ham United in 25 years thanks to a wonderful free-kick from flying Dutchman Martijn Reuser which kept Ipswich third in the Premiership.

WEDNESDAY 18TH MARCH 1981

Town moved comfortably into the semi-finals of the Uefa Cup at Portman Road with a 7-2 aggregate win over St Etienne. Second-half goals by Terry Butcher, John Wark and Paul Mariner saw them home with the French consolation coming from Jacques Zimako.

TUESDAY 18TH MARCH 1987

Zambian-born striker Neil Gregory scored a 37-minute hat-trick as the Blues brushed aside Sheffield United 3-1 at Portman Road. He plundered his first goal after only 19 seconds.

SATURDAY 19TH MARCH 1949

Belfast-born winger Jackie Brown plundered a hat-trick as Port Vale were battered 4-1 at Portman Road in Division Three (South).

SUNDAY 19TH MARCH 1961

Versatile defender Kevin Steggles was born in Ditchingham, Suffolk. Never an automatic choice, he only scored 2 goals in 61 games before joining West Bromwich Albion in 1987.

WEDNESDAY 20TH MARCH 1974

Ipswich crashed out of the Uefa Cup quarter-finals after losing 4-3 on penalties to East German outfit Lokomotiv Liepzig in Germany. Town hung on despite Mick Mills' dismissal in the first half and finally exited when Irishman Allan Hunter missed the crucial penalty.

MONDAY 20TH MARCH 1995

Midfield legend John Wark became the first-ever Blues player to be sent off against Norwich City in a 3-0 Premier League defeat at Carrow Road. It was George Burley's first game against the Canaries as manager.

SATURDAY 20TH MARCH 2004

Teenager Dean Bowditch scored a hat-trick live on Sky TV as the Tractor Boys beat Watford 4-1 at Portman Road. Jermaine Wright scored the other.

WEDNESDAY 21ST MARCH 1953

Millwall won 6-1 to inflict a record home defeat which would stand for 49 years. A paltry crowd of 9,373 saw Tommy Parker score Town's goal.

SATURDAY 21ST MARCH 1964

A fortnight after being crushed 6-0 at Liverpool, Jackie Milburn's men went down 9-1 at Stoke City in Division One. Dennis Viollet, who survived the Munich air disaster, scored a hat-trick.

SATURDAY 21ST MARCH 1970

Trevor Whymark scored the first of his 104 Blues goals in a 2-0 Portman Road stroll over Sunderland. Whymark, who scored four goals in a match three times for Town, also won an England cap against Luxembourg and joined Vancouver Whitecaps after 335 games.

WEDNESDAY 21ST MARCH 1979

A mammoth crowd of 100,000 at the Nou Camp – the joint biggest crowd Ipswich have played before – saw Barcelona win 1-0 and go through to the European Cup Winners' Cup fourth round.

SATURDAY 21ST MARCH 1981

Town's 2-1 defeat at Manchester United was their first defeat in twenty games. Terry Butcher grabbed Ipswich's goal in front of 46,685 fans.

WEDNESDAY 22ND MARCH 1939

Wing-half George Dougan was born in Glasgow. Signed from non-league Yiewsley Town, Dougan made only 17 league appearances before leaving to ply his trade in South Africa.

SATURDAY 22ND MARCH 2008

Right-sided schemer Danny Simpson, signed on loan from Manchester United, made his debut in a 2-1 victory at Scunthorpe United which saw Pablo Counago score and later dismissed for fighting.

MONDAY 23RD MARCH 1914

Livewire winger John Roy was born in Southampton. Roy started his career at Town's rivals Norwich City and later made 17 outings for the Blues over two seasons.

SATURDAY 23RD MARCH 1963

Jimmy Leadbetter's goal saw Ipswich climb out of the First Division relegation places with a win in their first-ever game at Old Trafford in front of 32,798 supporters.

THURSDAY 24TH MARCH 1892

Preston North End were the first professional club to play at Portman Road. A Suffolk County side, including three Town men in Notcutt, Haward and Kent, were defeated 3-0.

SATURDAY 24TH MARCH 2001

Icelandic defender Hermann Hreidarsson scored but his side went down 2-1 to Bulgaria in a World Cup qualifier.

WEDNESDAY 25TH MARCH 1953

A 1-0 home defeat to Leyton Orient in Division Three (South) was watched by 3,116 fans; the lowest ever League crowd at Portman Road.

SATURDAY 25TH MARCH 1967

South-African born Colin Viljoen marked his debut in some style with a home hat-trick as Ipswich pipped Portsmouth 4-2. Outrageously skilful but injury-plagued, Viljoen scored 54 goals in 372 appearances and won two caps for England in an eleven-year career.

TUESDAY 25TH MARCH 1969

Exciting right-winger John Miller became the first West Indian to be signed as a professional by the Blues. He made his debut in a 0-0 draw at Coventry City and made 60 appearances.

SATURDAY 25TH MARCH 1972

Bobby Robson's electric razor was stolen from the Town coach as they went down 1-0 at Leicester City.

WEDNESDAY 26TH MARCH 1986

A home crowd of only 4,476 saw goalkeeper Paul Cooper's testimonial: a 1-0 defeat to Norwich City. Cooper lasted only nine minutes before succumbing to a hamstring injury.

WEDNESDAY 26TH MARCH 2008

Macedonian midfield general Veliche Shumulikoski – signed for £500,000 from Turkish outfit Bursaspor – was booked in a 2-2 friendly draw in Bosnia-Herzegovina.

THURSDAY 27TH MARCH 1969

Wiry left-winger Stuart Slater was born in Sudbury. Never a prolific scorer, the £750,000 signing from Celtic was best running at defenders in a free role behind the strikers. An injury-ridden stay at Portman Road saw him play 88 games before leaving for Watford.

MONDAY 27TH MARCH 1978

A full house at Portman Road witnessed a Division One demolition job as local rivals Norwich City came a cropper 4-0 thanks to strikes from Brian Talbot (2), David Geddis and Mick Mills.

SATURDAY 28TH MARCH 1992

A brace from Jason Dozzell saw Town continue their bid to become Division Two champions as Derby County were seen off 2-1 at Portman Road.

SATURDAY 28TH MARCH 1998

The Blues stayed in the play-off frame with a 1-0 home win over Reading. Future loanee Andy Legg, and ex-Town hardman Andy Bernal, were both sent off for the visitors thanks to second yellow cards.

TUESDAY 29TH MARCH 2005

Darren Bent was replaced by Darren Ambrose as England under-21s beat their Azerbaijan counterparts 2-0 at Middlesbrough.

SATURDAY 29TH MARCH 2008

Town inched back into the Championship play-off spaces despite squandering a host of opportunities in a goalless draw with Queens Park Rangers at Portman Road. Owen Garvan and Danny Haynes both hit the woodwork.

WEDNESDAY 30TH MARCH 1960

Town forward Dermot Curtis scored as Ireland beat Chile 2-0 in a friendly at Dalymount Park, Dublin.

WEDNESDAY 30TH MARCH 1977

Paul Mariner made his England debut as a second-half replacement for Joe Royle as England thrashed Luxembourg 5-0 in front of 81,000 fans at Wembley in a World Cup qualifier.

SATURDAY 31ST MARCH 1951

Stirling-born winger Jimmy Roberts scored in a 1-1 draw at Bristol Rovers. It was the first time Town had drawn in 28 games.

SUNDAY 31ST MARCH 1968

Cambridge University educated Steve Palmer was born in Brighton. A reliable and hard-working midfielder, Palmer was a useful squad player for Town before departing to Watford for £135,000 after making 131 appearances and scoring 3 goals.

TUESDAY 31ST MARCH 1970

A marvellous fight back saw Arsenal defeated 2-1 at Portman Road as Division One relegation fears subsided. Billy Baxter and Frank Clarke plundered the all-important goals.

IPSWICH TOWN
On This Day

APRIL

SATURDAY 1st APRIL 1950

Town made fools out of Walsall in a Division Three (South) 3-1 win at Fellows Park. The victory came courtesy of goals from Ted Pole (2) and Sam McCrory. Local lad Pole ended his Town career with 13 goals in 40 games.

WEDNESDAY 1st APRIL 1987

England beat Northern Ireland – who included Town striker Kevin Wilson in their line up. Bobby Robson's side won 1-0 in a European Championship qualifier in Belfast.

THURSDAY 2nd APRIL 1925

Centre-forward Ron Blackman was born in Portsmouth. Blackman, a Reading legend with 158 Royals goals, scored 12 times over 3 seasons.

MONDAY 2nd APRIL 2001

Southampton were trounced 3-0 at The Dell as the Tractor Boys moved up to third in the Premier League in front of the Sky cameras. Marcus Stewart's hat-trick was the first in the top-flight for 16 years.

SATURDAY 3rd APRIL 1982

During half-time in a 1-0 home win over Coventry City, members from 9th Ipswich Deben Cubs had a brew up in the centre circle as part of a Cub competition to make tea in unusual places.

SATURDAY 3rd APRIL 1999

The Blues matched their highest away league victory with a 6-0 mauling of Swindon Town. George Burley's men stayed second in Division One after Craig Taylor was sent off for the Robins after six minutes.

FRIDAY 4th APRIL 1947

Town lost 4-3 at bottom club Mansfield Town at Field Mill in Division Three (South). The Blues were four goals down at the break but their storming fight back was not enough to get them a point.

SATURDAY 4th APRIL 1953

Walsall were pulverised 5-0 in Division Three (South) – a record win for the Blues against the Saddlers in 35 competitive games.

WEDNESDAY 4TH APRIL 1962

Town hotshot Ray Crawford scored his only England goal as Walter Winterbottom's men crushed Austria 3-1 at Wembley.

SATURDAY 5TH APRIL 1980

Ipswich moved third in the First Division as they despatched Norwich City 4-2 at Portman Road. The game marked John Wark's first hat-trick.

SUNDAY 5TH APRIL 1998

A 2-1 loss at Nottingham Forest was a first defeat in 22 Division One games – a brilliant run which took the Blues to eventual play-off misery against Charlton Athletic.

TUESDAY 5TH APRIL 2005

The Tractor Boys moved three points clear in the Championship promotion spots and relegated Rotherham United in a 4-3 victory at Portman Road. Darren Bent (2), Ian Westlake and Jim Magilton netted.

THURSDAY 6TH APRIL 1967

Mark Venus, a popular left-footed defender, was born in Hartlepool. Venus joined from Wolverhampton Wanderers, in a move which saw Steve Sedgley go in the opposite direction. His lethal set pieces saw him grab 19 goals in six years.

SATURDAY 6TH APRIL 2002

Relegation from the Premiership loomed large as Bolton Wanderers, inspired by German striker Fredi Bobic's first-half hat-trick, ran riot in a 4-1 Reebok Stadium victory.

SATURDAY 7TH APRIL 1979

Keeper Paul Cooper injured his hand late in the first-half in a 1-1 draw at Leeds United. He was replaced by winger Clive Woods, who took over until the break, before Cooper returned for the second half.

SATURDAY 7TH APRIL 1990

Winger Mark Stuart, on loan from Plymouth Argyle, scored twice in the first-half on his Town debut in a 3-3 Division Two draw at Watford.

SATURDAY 8TH APRIL 1978

Town travelled to Highbury to face West Bromwich Albion in the FA Cup semi-final hoping to clinch their first appearance in the final of football's most famous domestic cup competition. Brian Talbot's header went in off the bar to give the Blues an early lead. Unfortunately, the industrious midfielder had to be taken off with a head wound as a result of his bravery. Skipper Mick Mills then struck the second on 20 minutes from Mick Lambert's corner as a Wembley day out looked a certainty. However, the plucky Baggies reduced arrears with a Tony Brown penalty and it wasn't until the 86th minute that John Wark's thumping header booked Ipswich's ticket to London and a date with hot favourites Arsenal.

WEDNESDAY 8TH APRIL 1981

Despite tremendous Ipswich pressure throughout, the Blues could only register a 1-0 victory against a dogged and defensive FC Cologne outfit in the Uefa Cup semi-final first leg tie at Portman Road. The Germans, fielding England striker Tony Woodcock, capitulated to John Wark's 12th goal of the competition – a firm header on 33 minutes from Mick Mills' well-flighted cross.

MONDAY 8TH APRIL 1985

Ipswich managed their first League win in six years at Carrow Road, doing the double over Norwich City with a 2-0 win. Terry Butcher and Mich D'Avray scored as City had Asa Hartford sent off.

TUESDAY 9TH APRIL 1895

At a special meeting of Ipswich Town Football Club, the chance to move into professional football was turned down due to costs and the fact that football was to be 'played for fun and not become a business'. RD Hendry, a local businessman, was the lone voice to propose Town employ a professional team but was not successful.

WEDNESDAY 9TH APRIL 1975

A bad day for Ipswich Town as they lost 2-1 to West Ham in the FA Cup semi-final replay at Stamford Bridge. Despite dominating from start to finish, and having two clear goals disallowed controversially by referee Clive Thomas, Town were denied a deserved Wembley appearance.

TUESDAY 10TH APRIL 1973

Bryan Hamilton's extra-time winner at Portman Road saw Ipswich progress to the Texaco Cup Final after a 2-1 aggregate win over Newcastle United. Norwich City awaited in the final.

SATURDAY 10TH APRIL 1976

FA Cup finalists Manchester United were brought down to earth in Suffolk as they were thumped 3-0 thanks to strikes from Dave Johnson, Trevor Whymark and Mick Lambert in Division One.

SATURDAY 11TH APRIL 1953

Doug 'Dai' Rees scored his only Ipswich Town goal in 386 appearances in the 2-2 draw at Shrewsbury Town.

THURSDAY 11TH APRIL 1974

Matt Holland, born in Bury, was a magnificent Ipswich Town servant in a career spanning six seasons. After 314 outings and 45 goals, Holland joined Charlton Athletic but left a lasting impression after signing from AFC Bournemouth in August 1997.

FRIDAY 12TH APRIL 1963

Ipswich registered their first-ever win at Upton Park defeating the hosts 3-1 with goals from Doug Moran, Ray Crawford and Ted Phillips in a Division One clash watched by 23,170.

SATURDAY 12TH APRIL 2003

A marvellous second-half performance saw the Blues eclipse Coventry City 4-2 at Highfield Road and keep them in the play-off race. Marcus Bent and Pablo Counago both scored twice after Town trailed at the break.

SATURDAY 13TH APRIL 1968

Town kept up their Division Two title charge with a 2-0 home win over Rotherham United thanks to Ray Crawford's brace.

SUNDAY 13TH APRIL 2008

The Tractor Boys kept their Championship play-off hopes alive with a comfortable 2-1 victory over Norwich City. Roared on by 29,656 fans, goals from Danny Haynes, and an Alex Pearce own-goal, saw Town home.

MONDAY 14TH APRIL 1975

England under-21 goalkeeper Andy Marshall was born in Bury St Edmunds. Marshall was signed from Norwich City in the summer of 2001 but an injury saw his place taken by Italian Matteo Sereni. Marshall left Portman Road after playing 65 games.

SATURDAY 14TH APRIL 2007

Feisty defender Alex Bruce and future Blues loanee Stephen Bywater were sent off for fighting after 28 minutes as Derby County lost 2-1 in Suffolk.

SATURDAY 15TH APRIL 1995

Ian Marshall's strike prompted mass celebrations amongst the visiting fans in a 4-1 Premiership reverse at Arsenal. In a miserable season, it was Town's first goal in 675 minutes!

SATURDAY 15TH APRIL 2006

Despite a 2-1 Portman Road loss to Brighton & Hove Albion, Nicky Forster's goal saw him embark on a run of scoring in five straight games.

MONDAY 16TH APRIL 1973

A 1-1 draw at Bristol City was enough for Ipswich to win the FA Youth Cup for the first time. John Peddelty's goal ensured a 4-1 aggregate win.

WEDNESDAY 16TH APRIL 1975

Kevin Beattie made his England debut as Wembley witnessed a 5-0 crushing of Cyprus in a European Championship qualifier.

MONDAY 16TH APRIL 1979

Battling midfielder Sixto Peralta was born in Comodoro, Argentina. Signed on a year's loan from Inter Milan, Peralta became an instant hit with the Town faithful due to his never-say-die attitude and eye for goal. He set up Alun Armstrong's Uefa Cup winner against his employers in a famous Portman Road victory.

SATURDAY 17TH APRIL 1976

Ipswich notched a fourth successive league win over Arsenal, winning 2-1 at Highbury thanks to goals from Irishman Pat Sharkey and Enfield-born Keith Bertschin.

WEDNESDAY 17TH APRIL 2002

Fiery defender Amir Karic started for Slovenia as they defeated Tunisia 1-0 in a friendly. Karic was signed from FC Maribor for £700,000 but left after failing to start a game.

SATURDAY 18TH APRIL 1998

Dutch winger Bobby Petta scored twice in a 5-1 Division One demolition of Port Vale at Portman Road. Petta, who joined Town on a free transfer from Dutch giants Feyenoord in 1996, later had spells at Celtic and Fulham.

SATURDAY 18TH APRIL 1981

Goals from Charlie Nicholas and Kenny Sansom led Arsenal to a 2-0 victory at Portman Road in Division One and ended a run of 46 Portman Road games undefeated for Town.

SATURDAY 19TH APRIL 1947

Suffolk-born Ted Pole scored for the fifth straight game as Town beat Bournemouth & Boscombe Athletic 2-1 at Portman Road in Division Three (South).

MONDAY 19TH APRIL 1993

Town picked up a vital 3-1 Premiership win against Norwich City in front of the Sky cameras at Portman Road. Jason Dozzell's turn and long-range finish bagged the points for the battling Blues.

SATURDAY 20TH APRIL 1974

'Super' Paul Cooper made his Ipswich debut in a 3-2 defeat at champions-elect Leeds United at Elland Road. The Cannock-born stopper signed for a paltry £23,000 from Birmingham City and registered 575 first-team outings over twelve seasons. Cooper became an expert at saving penalties – keeping out 19 from a total of 49 spot kicks – and was desperately unlucky never to be capped by England.

TUESDAY 20TH APRIL 1982

Goalkeeper John Jackson marked his only Ipswich game with a 2-1 home win over mighty Manchester United. He was signed due to a glut of injuries at the age of 40 and left Town to join Hereford United and later Brighton & Hove Albion where he settled down after football to install blinds.

TUESDAY 21st APRIL 1970

A marvellous 3-2 victory over runners-up Leeds United at Portman Road saw Ipswich avoid relegation from the First Division. Jimmy Robertson (2) and Frank Clarke netted.

SATURDAY 21st APRIL 1973

Town's youth team received a tremendous ovation as they paraded the recently-won FA Youth Cup before a 2-1 Portman Road victory over Wolverhampton Wanderers.

SATURDAY 21st APRIL 1984

Ipswich's 3-0 away victory over basement dwellers Wolverhampton Wanderers was watched by just 6,611 people. It was the lowest attendance at Molineux for 47 years.

MONDAY 22nd APRIL 1957

Goals from Ted Phillips (2) and Jimmy Leadbetter on Easter Monday in a 3-1 win over Norwich City moved Ipswich to the top of Division Three (South) where they would remain. City were consigned to last place and an embarrassing re-election to the Football League.

WEDNESDAY 22nd APRIL 1981

Ipswich booked their place in the Uefa Cup Final with a sterling performance from the defence against Cologne in Germany. A makeshift Town back-line held firm and with the game approaching its final half hour, Terry Butcher headed Mick Mills' curling free-kick past a startled Schumacher to send the hosts into stunned silence. It ensured a first European final for the Town against AZ Alkmaar.

FRIDAY 22nd APRIL 2005

Town's youngsters won the FA Youth Cup for the third time in their history thanks to a 3-2 aggregate win over Southampton. Ed Upson scored the vital winning goal.

TUESDAY 23rd APRIL 1907

Stout-hearted centre-back Charles Cowie was born in Falkirk. His Football League debut was a forgettable 4-1 home reverse to Newport County. He appeared in six more League games before joining the army.

SATURDAY 23RD APRIL 1988

A blistering hat-trick from jet-heeled striker Dalian Atkinson saw the Blues destroy Middlesbrough 4-0 at Portman Road in Division Two. Boro featured future Ipswich caretaker-manager Tony Mowbray in their ranks.

MONDAY 24TH APRIL 1961

The Blues clinched the Second Division championship by destroying Derby County 4-1 at the Baseball Ground, despite trailing at the interval. Roy Stephenson (2), Ray Crawford and Dermot Curtis were the heroes.

SATURDAY 24TH APRIL 1976

Derby County won 6-2 at Portman Road on the final day of the season. Town finished sixth in Division One.

SATURDAY 24TH APRIL 1999

Bottom club Crewe Alexandra picked up a shock 2-1 win at Portman Road despite future Town midfielder Jermaine Wright being dismissed on 77 minutes for a second yellow card.

SATURDAY 25TH APRIL 1953

A 2-0 defeat at Swindon Town in Division Three (South) would be the last occasion the Blues would draw a blank for 33 consecutive games.

SATURDAY 25TH APRIL 1992

A momentous day saw Town book a place in the inaugural Premier League the following season. A 1-1 draw at Oxford United cemented promotion from Division Two, Gavin Johnson levelling an earlier strike from future Town boss Jim Magilton.

MONDAY 26TH APRIL 1954

Town clinched the Division Three (South) title with a 2-1 victory at Newport County. A crowd of 11,258 in Wales saw Tom Garneys and Willie Callaghan cap promotion for the Blues.

WEDNESDAY 26TH APRIL 1995

Elegant midfielder Claus Thomsen made his Denmark debut in a 1-0 victory over Macedonia in Copenhagen.

JOHN LYALL WATCHES TOWN WIN PROMOTION AT OXFORD IN APRIL 1992

SATURDAY 27TH APRIL 1963

Alf Ramsey's final game in charge of Town before becoming England manager ended in a 2-1 victory over Burnley in Suffolk. Ramsey won three championships in his Portman Road spell.

SATURDAY 27TH APRIL 1996

Alex Mathie's goal at Fratton Park saw Ipswich maintain a Division One play-off place. The 1-0 win extended Town's 30-year unbeaten run at Portsmouth.

SATURDAY 28TH APRIL 1951

A 3-1 win at Carrow Road broke Norwich City's unbroken home record and condemned the hosts to runners-up spot in Division Three (South). Peter Dobson and Sam McCrory (2) scored.

SATURDAY 28TH APRIL 1962

A momentous date in Ipswich Town history as a 2-0 Portman Road victory over Aston Villa saw the Blues crowned Champions of the Football League at the first attempt. Burnley's goalless draw with Chelsea, combined with Ray Crawford's brace, sent 28,932 fans home delirious.

SATURDAY 29TH APRIL 1922

Town registered their first major championship title with a 2-1 win at runners-up Eastbourne. Arthur Fenn's brace secured the Southern Amateur League; 4,000 fans welcomed the Blues at Ipswich station that night.

SATURDAY 29TH APRIL 1950

On a miserable day, Belfast-born inside-forward Sam McCrory became the first Ipswich player to be sent off since Town joined the Football League in a 5-0 drubbing at Aldershot.

SATURDAY 30TH APRIL 1938

Goal-machine Gilbert Alsop scored four goals as Town pulverised Aldershot Town reserves 7-0 in the Southern League.

WEDNESDAY 30TH APRIL 1975

Ipswich won the FA Youth Cup for the second time in three years thanks to a 2-0 second leg Portman Road win over West Ham United watched by 16,278. They triumphed 5-1 over the two games.

IPSWICH TOWN
On This Day

MAY

FRIDAY 1st MAY 1936

At a Special General Meeting at the Town Hall, a resolution was passed to amalgamate Ipswich Town and Ipswich United. Ipswich Town FC Ltd was formed and professional football finally arrived at Portman Road.

WEDNESDAY 1st MAY 1957

Town turned on a brilliant performance to beat Southampton 2-0 at The Dell and become Division Three (South) champions following goals from Basil Acres and Jimmy Leadbetter. Torquay United, needing to win, could only draw 1-1 at Crystal Palace and Alf Ramsey's men could celebrate.

WEDNESDAY 1st MAY 1963

Jackie Milburn, player-coach at Yiewsley, was appointed as successor to Alf Ramsey and took charge of affairs at Portman Road.

SATURDAY 1st MAY 1976

Bobby Stokes' shock late winner for Southampton over Manchester United in the FA Cup Final meant Town were denied a place in Europe despite finishing sixth in Division One – their lowest finish in four seasons.

FRIDAY 2nd MAY 1975

Town beat a Don Revie XI 5-3 in a testimonial match for Colin Harper watched by 15,174 spectators. Ipswich-born Harper was a solid left-back who joined Port Vale as player-coach after 180 games.

SATURDAY 2nd MAY 1992

John Lyall's men paraded the Division Two trophy and consigned Brighton & Hove Albion to the drop with a 3-1 win before 26,803 fans. Steve Whitton (2) and Gavin Johnson netted amidst a carnival atmosphere in Suffolk.

WEDNESDAY 3rd MAY 1961

Scotland beat Republic of Ireland 4-1 in their first-ever meeting as Irishman Dermot Curtis won his 14th cap at Hampden Park, Glasgow.

SATURDAY 3rd MAY 1986

Terry Butcher played for already-relegated Town for the last time in 1-0 defeat at Sheffield Wednesday. Butcher joined Glasgow Rangers for £275,000 after 351 appearances in eight years and 45 England caps while at Ipswich.

SATURDAY 4TH MAY 1963

Jackie Milburn's first game as Town gaffer saw the Blues draw 0-0 at Wolverhampton Wanderers. Milburn's woeful managerial spell was as follows: P 56, W 11, D 12 and L 33.

MONDAY 4TH MAY 1973

Mick Mills lifted the Texaco Cup for Ipswich as Norwich City were trumped 4-1 over two legs of football witnessed by nearly 60,000 fans. Town did not have an opportunity to defend the trophy due to Uefa Cup commitments the following season, having qualified for Europe several weeks before the victory.

SATURDAY 4TH MAY 1985

Twelve years later times had changed as Mick Mills made his 100th appearance for Southampton in a 3-0 defeat for Town at The Dell.

SUNDAY 4TH MAY 1997

Birmingham City's Paul Devlin netted in a 1-1 Division One draw at Portman Road, the first goal that the Blues had conceded in five games.

MONDAY 5TH MAY 1929

Outside-right Willie Jones was born in Aberbargoed, Wales. Jones signed for Ipswich in April 1949 and made his league debut against Crystal Palace the next season. Over the next three seasons, Jones made sporadic appearances and scored his one goal in a 2-2 draw with Colchester United.

SATURDAY 5TH MAY 1990

Scotsman John Duncan's final game as Ipswich manager ensured he ended on a high as the Blues won 3-1 at The Hawthorns thanks to goals from David Lowe, Simon Milton and Jason Dozzell. Duncan's tenure in Suffolk saw his side miss out on promotion to the top-flight for three successive seasons.

SUNDAY 5TH MAY 1996

Needing a win to clinch a play-off berth, Town could only draw 0-0 with Millwall in front of 17,290 increasingly desperate fans. Bury-born striker James Scowcroft came closest to breaking the deadlock with a header that hit the post as the Blues failed to score for the first time in 14 games.

SATURDAY 6TH MAY 1978

A date which should be etched in the consciousness of all Ipswich Town fans. The Blues, branded underdogs and poor country cousins by the majority of the media, beat Arsenal 1-0 in front of a Wembley crowd of 100,000, and a TV audience of millions, to lift the FA Cup for the first time in their history. Roger Osborne's 77th-minute strike, and subsequent substitution due to exhaustion, was the pinnacle of a tremendous performance by Town who hit the woodwork three times and totally dominated the North London giants. The winning goal was created by youngster David Geddis whose twisting run and low cross was only cleared by Arsenal's Willie Young to Osborne lurking eight yards out. His clinical finish prompted Brian Moore's infamous 'Osborne, 1-0!' comment and pandemonium amongst the Blue hordes in Wembley, Suffolk and many places beyond.

WEDNESDAY 6TH MAY 1981

Exactly three years to the day after the famous FA Cup Final victory, another memorable chapter in the history of Ipswich Town was written. Facing Dutch champions AZ 67 Alkmaar at a bouncing Portman Road, the Blues emphatically won 3-0 in the first leg of the Uefa Cup Final to give themselves a great chance of claiming their first piece of European silverware. A surprisingly rugged, cynical Dutch side were swept aside and trailed at half-time thanks to a John Wark penalty. Outwitted by fellow countrymen Muhren and Thijssen, the visitors were undone by two simple goals within 10 minutes of the second half. Thijssen headed home after his shot was parried and then Alan Brazil's brilliant cross was flicked home by Mariner as Town set themselves up for the second leg in Amsterdam.

MONDAY 7TH MAY 1984

Town avoided relegation from Division One with a fantastic fight back to beat Manchester United 2-1 at Old Trafford. Inspired signing Alan Sunderland scored one while Mich D'Avray's late winner was watched by 44,257 stunned fans.

SATURDAY 7TH MAY 1994

Pint-size Mark Stein's injury-time winner for Chelsea against Sheffield United at Stamford Bridge meant the Blades were relegated instead of Ipswich on the final day of the Premiership season.

TOWN'S 1981 UEFA CUP-WINNING SQUAD CONTINUE THEIR ROLLERCOASTER RIDE

MONDAY 8TH MAY 1939

First Division Aston Villa defeated Town 3-2 in The Ipswich Hospital Cup in front of a crowd of 20,000 which raised £1,200 for the East Suffolk and Ipswich Hospital. Villa's Scottish international Frank O'Donnell netted a five-minute hat-trick.

SATURDAY 8TH MAY 1976

Genial midfielder Pat Sharkey won his only Northern Ireland cap in a 3-0 Glasgow drubbing by Scotland.

FRIDAY 9TH MAY 1924

Joe O'Brien was a lightning quick left-winger born in Dublin. O'Brien scored 11 goals in his debut 1949/50 season at Portman Road.

SUNDAY 9TH MAY 1999

Town had to make do with a third successive place in the play-offs despite destroying Sheffield United 4-1 at Portman Road. Goals from James Scowcroft, Jim Magilton, Keiron Dyer and Richard Naylor were not enough as Bradford City managed to win at Wolverhampton Wanderers to claim automatic promotion.

TUESDAY 10TH MAY 1920

Town, still an amateur side, claimed a bit of a scalp when they defeated First Division Chelsea 1-0 in front of a then record crowd of 8,000 at Portman Road. Len Mitzen's fine shot on 55 minutes gave Town a famous win in a charity match made possible by Earl Cadogan's friendship with the London side.

WEDNESDAY 10TH MAY 1950

Town gain local bragging rights as they won the Norfolk Jubilee Cup with a 2-1 victory over East Anglian rivals Norwich City at Portman Road. John Elsworthy's header and a wonderful volley from Stan Parker clinched the win.

SATURDAY 10TH MAY 1997

Mick Stockwell's late equaliser at Sheffield United made Town favourites for the second leg of the Division One play-off semi-final. Welshman Geraint Williams set up Stockwell's goal with a clever pass.

TUESDAY 11TH MAY 1968

Town's point at home against Blackburn Rovers, thanks to Ray Crawford's header, was enough to win the Second Division title and ensured Town's fifth championship win in fifteen years.

TUESDAY 11TH MAY 1976

Mick Mills was to win the bragging rights over fellow Blues defender Allan Hunter as England thumped Northern Ireland 4-0 in a Home Championships encounter.

FRIDAY 11TH MAY 1979

By beating Queens Park Rangers 4-0 at Loftus Road, Town moved above Arsenal and guaranteed a place in the Uefa Cup for the next season. Terry Butcher scored and marked former Blue Paul Goddard out of the game.

SATURDAY 11TH MAY 1991

Despite Chris Kiwomya's goal, John Lyall's men finished 14th in Division Two after a 2-1 reverse at Brighton & Hove Albion. It was the club's worst league placing for 25 years.

MONDAY 12TH MAY 1947

FA Cup winners Charlton Athletic came to Portman Road for the Ipswich Hospital Cup. A 2-2 draw attracted a season-high crowd of 22,012.

SATURDAY 12TH MAY 1984

The Blues finished the season firmly mid-table in Division One. They continued a six-match unbeaten run by beating Aston Villa 2-1 in Suffolk. Eric Gates and Mich D'Avray scored.

WEDNESDAY 13TH MAY 1981

Town lost only their second league game at Portman Road that season as they lost out to Southampton 3-2. Only a week before they would travel to Holland for the Uefa Cup Final second leg, a strong team went down despite strikes from John Wark and Alan Brazil.

SATURDAY 13TH MAY 1989

John Wark's brace in a 2-0 home win over Blackburn Rovers meant Ipswich Town finished eighth in Division Two, ending with five straight wins.

THURSDAY 14TH MAY 1987

Town's first play-off appearance ended 0-0 at home to Charlton Athletic at Portman Road. The Blues had finished fifth in Division Two while the Londoners were placed 19th in Division One.

WEDNESDAY 14TH MAY 1997

More play-off woe as Town were defeated on the away goal rule by Sheffield United despite a 2-2 draw at Portman Road. They had already done the double over the Blades in the league with two 3-1 victories. Strikes from James Scowcroft and Niklas Gudmundsson were not enough.

SUNDAY 14TH MAY 2000

A record of just one win in eight play-off games was ignored as a tidy Blues performance, crowned by two marvellous goals from Marcus Stewart, saw them claim a creditable 2-2 draw against Bolton Wanderers at the Reebok Stadium in the semi-final first leg.

WEDNESDAY 15TH MAY 1968

Defender Tommy Carroll made his Republic of Ireland bow in a 2-2 draw with Poland. The Dublin-born right-back won 8 caps while at Portman Road and scored 3 goals in 126 games for Town.

SATURDAY 15TH MAY 1982

Peter Davenport's second-half hat-trick for Nottingham Forest meant Town lost their last game of a magnificent season 3-1. The Blues finished as runners-up to Liverpool who had also knocked out Town in the League Cup semi-finals.

MONDAY 16TH MAY 1966

Andy Bernal was a rugged Australian defender signed from Spanish club Sporting Gijon in September 1987 by John Duncan. He left Portman Road after just four starts but later forged a good career at Reading.

MONDAY 16TH MAY 1977

Town's chances of winning Division One were scuppered in a 1-0 defeat at Queens Park Rangers. The West Londoners ensured their own top-flight survival thanks to Irish international Don Givens who scored with a sweet left-foot shot.

MONDAY 17TH MAY 1982

Ipswich's most successful boss Bobby Robson ended his time in charge of Town with a 2-1 home win over Tottenham Hotspur; he left the club to replace Ron Greenwood as England manager. Robson won the FA Cup and the Uefa Cup as Town boss, and presided over a golden spell at the club which included 316 victories.

SUNDAY 17TH MAY 1987

Town's travelling army of 5,000 fans left the Valley distraught as Charlton Athletic triumphed 2-1 in the Division Two play-off semi-final second leg. Steve McCall's late goal was not enough to save Bobby Ferguson's job. He became the first Ipswich Town manager to be sacked.

WEDNESDAY 17TH MAY 2000

Jim Magilton's breathtaking hat-trick saw Town overcome their play-off hoodoo and reached Wembley for the first time since 1978 with a 5-3 second leg win over Bolton Wanderers. The Trotters had two men sent off as 21,543 fans turned Portman Road into a cauldron of noise.

TUESDAY 18TH MAY 1916

Outside-right Ambrose Mulraney was born in Wishaw, Scotland. Mulraney was a quick winger who could play on either flank. He achieved a goalscoring debut in the Football League against Walsall and has the distinction of netting Ipswich Town's first-ever hat-trick in the Football League as Bristol City were crushed 4-0.

WEDNESDAY 18TH MAY 1949

Ron Wigg, who scored 14 Town goals in 39 starts, was born in Dunmow. Signed from Leyton Orient in 1967, Wigg stayed at Portman Road for over two years before having successful spells at Watford and Rotherham United.

TUESDAY 18TH MAY 2004

West Ham United dumped the Blues out of the play-off semi-finals 2-1 on aggregate at Upton Park. The game was giant defender Matt Elliott's last in a Town shirt. Midfield schemer Ian Westlake's shot nearly silenced the home crowd but it smacked a post and bounced to safety.

FRIDAY 19TH MAY 1978

Towering frontman Marcus Bent was born in Hammersmith. Signed from Blackburn Rovers for £3m as cover for Marcus Stewart, Bent had to wait before making an impact with six goals in as many games. He joined Everton for £450,000 after scoring 23 goals for Town.

WEDNESDAY 19TH MAY 1999

A first-ever Town play-off victory saw Bolton Wanderers defeated 4-3 in extra time in Suffolk with goals from Matt Holland (2) and Keiron Dyer (2). The Trotters, however, sneaked through to the final on the away goals rule.

SATURDAY 20TH MAY 1922

Whippet racing was seen for the first time at Portman Road as groundsman Walter Wollard was forbidden to continue to keep fowl in the grandstand.

WEDNESDAY 20TH MAY 1981

The night that Town won the Uefa Cup in Amsterdam and flew back to Suffolk with their first European trophy! Boosted by 10,000 travelling fans and a seemingly comfortable 3-0 cushion from the first leg, Thijssen's fourth-minute half-volley sent the fans into ecstasy. However, AZ 67 Alkmaar were not going to take defeat lying down and stormed back at Ipswich, penning them in their half as they took the lead on the night with goals from Welzl and Metgod. John Wark's shot – meaning a joint record 14 goals in a European competition – gave Town a lifeline but Tol's goal on 40 minutes saw the hosts two goals behind with 45 minutes left. A second half battering from AZ eventually saw Jonker's free-kick fly past Cooper on 73 minutes but the defence held firm to the end. Skipper Mick Mills lifted the trophy amongst emotional scenes.

TUESDAY 21ST MAY 1963

A 1-1 draw with Aston Villa concluded Town's league campaign as English champions with a disappointing seventeenth placed finish. Doug Moran scored his eleventh goal of the campaign.

WEDNESDAY 21ST MAY 1975

England's 2-2 Home Championship draw with Wales at Wembley featured two Town players. David Johnson scored both goals on his England debut while Colin Viljoen gained his second and final cap.

MICK MILLS COLLECTS THE UEFA CUP IN MAY 1981

FRIDAY 22ND MAY 1953

Paul Mariner, who scored a total of 135 goals in 339 appearances, was born in Bolton. He was signed by Bobby Robson from Plymouth Argyle for £220,000 in 1976 and was to win Uefa Cup and FA Cup medals before joining Arsenal eight years later. Mariner won 33 England caps whilst at Ipswich and scored 14 goals for his country.

THURSDAY 22ND MAY 1969

Town went goal crazy in an end-of-season friendly with Morphou in Cyprus. Ron Wigg (5), Chris Barnard (3) and Bobby Hunt (2) led the frenzy.

THURSDAY 23RD MAY 1952

Canadian full-back Bruce Twamley was born. Twamley unfortunately broke his leg on his debut against Wolverhampton Wanderers and was to make only one more appearance in a Town shirt.

WEDNESDAY 23RD MAY 1979

NASL outfit Minnesota Kicks and Town played out a dull end-of-term draw in an International Challenge friendly at the host's Metropolitan Stadium.

SATURDAY 24TH MAY 1975

A wonderful day for Ipswich and England as David Johnson and Kevin Beattie both scored as England smashed Scotland 5-1 at Wembley before 98,241 fans.

SUNDAY 24TH MAY 1981

An open-topped bus drove the Blues' Uefa Cup winning victors and trophy through Ipswich to a civic reception at the Town Hall. Thousands of fans turned out to cheer them on a three-hour journey.

SATURDAY 25TH MAY 1963

Town went down 2-1 to an East Berlin XI in an end of season friendly watched by 70,000 fans. The game finished five minutes early so as not to clash with the end of the Prague-Warsaw-Berlin cycle race.

TUESDAY 25TH MAY 1982

Midfield maestro Arnold Muhren won his last Dutch cap as a Town player in a 2-0 defeat to England at Wembley

THURSDAY 26TH MAY 1932

Goalkeeper Roy Bailey was born in Epsom. Bailey's debut was a nightmare as he conceded two goals in the first three minutes against Norwich City in a 3-2 reverse. He eventually made 346 Town appearances between 1956 and 1964. His son, Gary, kept goal for Manchester United and won full England honours.

SATURDAY 26TH MAY 1979

John Wark scored his second goal for Scotland in a 3-1 drubbing from England in the Home Championships.

FRIDAY 27TH MAY 1932

Roy Stephenson, a flying right-winger, was born in Crook. Joining from Lowestoft Town in 1965, Stephenson scored 26 goals in 163 games and his accurate crossing assisted innumerable Ipswich goals.

THURSDAY 27TH MAY 1999

Forward David Johnson won his third Jamaican cap as his side lost 2-1 to Sweden in a friendly.

WEDNESDAY 28TH MAY 1980

Striker Alan Brazil made his Scottish debut as a substitute for Joe Jordan in a 0-0 friendly draw with Poland in Poznan. Brazil failed to score for Scotland in 11 appearances for his country whilst with Town.

FRIDAY 29TH MAY 1936

Mick O'Brien was appointed the first-ever manager of Ipswich Town. O'Brien had previously played for Norwich City, amongst other clubs, and joined as assistant manager from Brentford.

MONDAY 29TH MAY 2000

A magnificent 4-2 win over Barnsley at Wembley saw Town finally bury their play-off hoodoo and reach the Premiership. In a pulsating match on a sunny day, Tony Mowbray's header and Richard Wright's penalty save from Craig Hignett saw the sides go into the break level. A tremendous second-half display was crowned by goals from Richard Naylor, Marcus Stewart and Martijn Reuser to send the Ipswich faithful home ecstatic and ensure a marvellous climax to a wonderful season under George Burley.

MONDAY 30TH MAY 1938

A momentous day in Ipswich Town's history. At a meeting in London, it was announced that Town, with 36 votes, would be elected to the Football League for the following season. Exactly 60 years after Ipswich Association were formed, Ipswich Town would make their debut in professional league football and an amazing journey was to begin.

SATURDAY 31ST MAY 1947

Centre-half George Clarke scored on his debut as Town drew 2-2 at Northampton Town in the final Division Three (South) fixture that season. Clarke made a total of 37 appearances in six years before retiring.

SUNDAY 31ST MAY 1970

John Lyall signed Danish defender Claus Thomsen from Aarhus for £250,000 in June 1994. Thomsen was a cultured player who joined Everton for a profit after 8 goals in 97 Town outings.

IPSWICH TOWN
On This Day

JUNE

SATURDAY 1st JUNE 1963

Town won their third fixture of an end-of-season European tour with a 5-1 thrashing of Czechoslovakian First Division outfit Jednota Trecin. Ray Crawford's hat-trick in blistering sunshine was witnessed by 3,000.

SATURDAY 1st JUNE 2002

Midfielder Matt Holland scored a fine goal as Republic of Ireland drew 1-1 with Cameroon in their opening World Cup finals game in Niigata, Japan.

FRIDAY 2nd JUNE 1972

Elegant central defender John McGreal was born in Birkenhead. The £650,000 capture from Tranmere Rovers immediately settled at Portman Road and his strong tackling and crisp passing impressed many. He eventually joined Burnley after five years of sterling service and 150 appearances in a Town shirt.

SUNDAY 2nd JUNE 2002

Town left-back Amir Karic, on loan to NK Maribor at the time, was booked as Slovenia crashed 3-1 to Spain in a World Cup finals group game in Gwangju, South Korea.

FRIDAY 3rd JUNE 1977

Town kicked-off a summer tour to Canada with a 1-0 victory at Toronto Metros-Croatia who had just won the NASL Atlantic Conference.

TUESDAY 3rd JUNE 1986

Portugal beat England 1-0 in Monterrey as the latter began their World Cup finals campaign in Mexico. Terry Butcher, who would leave Town for Rangers on his return, played and would start in every game in the tournament.

WEDNESDAY 4th JUNE 2003

Mauritanian Drissa Diallo, a tough, though injury-prone centre-back, was signed from Burnley on a free transfer. Diallo made 49 appearances before joining Sheffield Wednesday.

WEDNESDAY 4th JUNE 2008

Tiny Town winger Jaime Peters headed his first international goal on his 14th appearance for Canada in a 2-2 draw with Panama in a Florida friendly.

WEDNESDAY 5TH JUNE 1963

Slovakian outfit Kosice defeated a weary Town side 4-2 in their final game of a five-match tour. The Blues led at half-time thanks to goals from Bobby Blackwood and Ray Crawford but capitulated after the break.

MONDAY 5TH JUNE 2006

Jim Magilton, former Town midfielder and Northern Ireland skipper, was appointed the surprise successor to Joe Royle and charged with returning the Blues to the Premiership. Magilton's playing career spanned eight seasons and the creative and smooth-passing creative midfielder scored 21 goals in 315 games.

MONDAY 6TH JUNE 1966

Nottingham-born David Hill was a tireless, left-sided player signed by John Duncan from Scunthorpe United for £90,000. He made 71 Town appearances but never scored despite being a skilful free-kick specialist.

FRIDAY 6TH JUNE 2008

Reggie Lambe, a Town Academy midfielder, won his fourth Bermudan cap as the hosts beat Barbados 2-1 in a friendly.

MONDAY 7TH JUNE 1937

Town, with 24 votes, were unsuccessful with their first application to play in the Football League. Exeter City (40 votes) and Aldershot City (34 votes) were re-elected to the Third Division South instead.

THURSDAY 7TH JUNE 1979

George Burley and John Wark both starred as Jock Stein's Scotland beat Norway 4-0 in a European Championship qualifier in Oslo.

SATURDAY 8TH JUNE 1957

Shot-stopper Charlie Ashcroft joined Coventry City after seven appearances. Ashcroft was unable to displace goalkeeping legend Roy Bailey whom Alf Ramsey had bought a year earlier.

WEDNESDAY 8TH JUNE 1977

Battling midfielder Brian Talbot picked up his third England cap in a 0-0 friendly draw with Brazil at The Maracana.

TUESDAY 9TH JUNE 1936

Ipswich were elected to the Southern League – the first professional league that they were to play in. Manager Mick O'Brien was instructed to start signing players immediately.

TUESDAY 9TH JUNE 1987

Creative midfielder Jason Dozzell won his fourth England under-21 cap in a 0-0 draw with the USSR.

SUNDAY 10TH JUNE 1973

Born on this day in Clarmont Farrand, France, hard-working midfielder Sylvain Legwinski joined the Blues from Fulham on a free transfer in August 2006. The popular leader scored seven goals at Portman Road and made a good impression before leaving the club.

WEDNESDAY 10TH JUNE 1981

Town went down 2-1 to NASL side Calgary Bloomers, then owned by Canadian businessman Nelson Skalbania – famous for signing 17-year-old future ice hockey legend Wayne Gretzky to the World Hockey Association.

TUESDAY 11TH JUNE 1935

John Laurel, an England youth international centre-half, was born in Dartford. Laurel did not make an appearance for Tottenham Hotspur before joining Town in the summer of 1959. His debut was a 5-2 first-ever victory at Leeds United. Laurel made five more starts before joining non-league King's Lynn.

SATURDAY 11TH JUNE 1977

Allan Hunter won his 37th Northern Ireland cap as his side went down to Iceland 1-0 in a World Cup Qualifier in Reykjavik.

TUESDAY 12TH JUNE 1923

Jimmy Roberts, who joined Town from Dundee in 1949, was born in Stirling. The tricky left-winger made 81 appearances and notched 17 goals before joining Barrow in the Third Division (North).

SUNDAY JUNE 12TH 1983

England, managed by Bobby Robson, drew 0-0 in Sydney against Australia in a friendly. Russell Osman and Terry Butcher were the centre-back pairing.

WEDNESDAY 13TH JUNE 1979

Creative Irish midfielder Alan Quinn was born in Dublin. Quinn started off at non-league Cherry Orchard before spells at Sheffield Wednesday and Sunderland. Town signed him for £400,000 from Sheffield United after a successful loan spell.

SUNDAY 13TH JUNE 2004

Giant defender Jason De Vos won his 46th international cap as Canada trounced Belize 4-0 in a World Cup qualifier in Ontario.

SUNDAY 14TH JUNE 1977

Town drew 1-1 with Portland Timbers at the Canadian club's Civic Stadium in an end-of-season friendly. The Timbers featured former West Ham striker Clyde Best, one of the first post-World War II black players to appear in English football.

MONDAY 14TH JUNE 1980

Frans Thijssen became the first Town player to appear at the European Championships as his Dutch side lost 3-2 to West Germany in Naples.

MONDAY 15TH JUNE 1936

Oswald Parry was signed as Ipswich Town's first ever professional player. The tough-tackling full-back joined from Crystal Palace and made 104 league appearances.

TUESDAY 15TH JUNE 1980

Italy beat England 1-0 in Naples as Paul Mariner appeared as a late substitute for Garry Birtles to become Town's first English representative at the European Championships.

TUESDAY 15TH JUNE 1982

John Wark became the first Town player to play in the World Cup finals, scoring two in three minutes, as Scotland beat New Zealand 5-2 in Malaga.

WEDNESDAY 16TH JUNE 1982

Terry Butcher had a hand in the fastest goal in World Cup finals history, nodding on a throw from Steve Coppell for Bryan Robson to score after 27 seconds in a 3-1 win over France. Mick Mills and Paul Mariner also played.

SUNDAY 16TH JUNE 2002

Republic of Ireland crashed out on penalties to Spain in a World Cup finals second round game in Japan. Matt Holland's penalty hit the crossbar as Spain triumphed 3-2.

THURSDAY 17TH JUNE 1927

Falkirk-born wing-half Neil Myles waited for four months to make his Town debut but netted twice in a 4-4 draw with Crystal Palace. He was a key factor when the Blues won the Division Three (South) title twice in the 1950s.

SATURDAY 17TH JUNE 1944

Town chairman, Lieutenant-Colonel Ivan Cobbold, was killed with some of his colleagues when a flying bomb hit the Guards Chapel in London during a service. Cobbold led the club into professionalism and was one of the club's greatest influences.

THURSDAY 18TH JUNE 1987

Dundee-born John Duncan was appointed as Town manager after leading Chesterfield to the Fourth Division championship two years before.

SUNDAY 18TH JUNE 1916

Winger Jackie Brownlow was born in Belfast. He only played one game for Town and on his debut set up Tommy Parker's goal against Aldershot with a pinpoint cross. He left Town to join Hartlepool where he made three appearances.

SUNDAY 19TH JUNE 1966

David Kerslake, a solid right-back touted as the 'next Duncan Edwards' as a youngster was born in Stepney. Town signed him from Tottenham Hotspur on a free transfer in 1997 but he couldn't break into the first team consistently and joined Swindon Town a year later.

WEDNESDAY 19TH JUNE 1996

Distinguished midfielder Claus Thomsen starred for Denmark as they crushed Turkey 3-0 at Hillsborough in the European Championship finals. Thomsen started in every game that Denmark played in the competition, hosted by England.

MATT HOLLAND MISSES FOR IRELAND AGAINST SPAIN IN JUNE 2002

SATURDAY 20TH JUNE 1964

Alec Chamberlain, a promising young goalkeeper spotted by Bobby Robson, was born in March, Cambridgeshire. Chamberlain, however, was released before making a Town appearance and joined Colchester United before enjoying a successful professional career with seven clubs.

FRIDAY 20TH JUNE 2003

Disastrous signing Ulrich Le Pen left Portman Road for Strasbourg on a free transfer. The French left-winger cost Town £1.4m from Rennes and never made a start in Suffolk after suffering a bad ankle injury on his debut.

TUESDAY 21ST JUNE 1955

Welsh wing-half Billy Baker was signed from Cardiff City. His brief career at Portman Road was highlighted by a run of 20 consecutive games as the club finished third in Division Three (South). Baker was a Japanese prisoner of war for four years in World War II.

SUNDAY 22ND JUNE 1913

John Dempsey, an inside-forward who scored two on his Town debut against Torquay United, was born in Cumbernauld. However, his promising career was curtailed by injury and he retired after just one season and five goals.

SUNDAY 22ND JUNE 1986

Diego Maradona's swerving, balletic run and fine finish past Terry Butcher and numerous other English tackles saw England knocked out of the World Cup finals. Maradona had earlier punched a goal past Peter Shilton – claiming he was assisted by the 'Hand of God'.

THURSDAY 23RD JUNE 1921

Jim Feeney, a stylish left-footed defender, was born in Belfast. Signed from Swansea Town, Feeney was a virtual ever-present for six seasons after making his debut in 1950. In his 232nd, and final, appearance against Brighton & Hove Albion he broke his nose after six minutes and had to be taken off.

FRIDAY 23RD JUNE 2006

Joe Royle signed striker Sam Parkin from Swindon Town for £450,000. The centre-forward failed to make an impression at Portman Road and left for Luton Town after scoring just five goals.

SATURDAY 24TH JUNE 1955

Tall goalkeeper Craig Forrest won his 28th international cap but was unable to prevent Canada losing 1-0 to Denmark in a Sky Dome Cup fixture in Toronto.

TUESDAY 24TH JUNE 2008

Former Town winger Brian Siddall passed away aged 78. Siddall, who scored on his Town debut, played 59 games for the Blues between 1957 and 1960.

FRIDAY 25TH JUNE 1987

Chelsea signed Ipswich goal-machine Kevin Wilson for a fee of £335,000. The striker went on to notch an impressive 55 goals in 155 starts for the Stamford Bridge outfit.

SATURDAY 25TH JUNE 1988

Arnold Muhren's magnificent cross field pass was volleyed brilliantly home by Marco van Basten as Holland beat Russia 2-0 in the European Championship Final in Munich.

THURSDAY 26TH JUNE 1969

Future Town striker Mick Lambert had the honour of being twelfth man for England in the Lord's test match against the West Indies. Opener Geoff Boycott scored an England century in a close draw.

TUESDAY 26TH JUNE 2007

Preston-born left-back Scott Barron left Town for Millwall on a free transfer. The hard-tackling defender never forced a run in the first team and made sixteen starts before leaving Suffolk.

SATURDAY 27TH JUNE 1942

Dave Bevis, a Southampton-born goalkeeper, never appeared on the winning side for Town in the six league games he played between 1963 and 1966. He left to play non-league football with Cambridge City.

FRIDAY 27TH JUNE 2008

Welsh midfielder Gavin Williams joined Championship rivals Bristol City for £100,000. The injury-plagued Williams scored on his Town debut but failed to settle at Portman Road after making 59 appearances.

TUESDAY 28TH JUNE 1955

Eric Lazenby Gates was born in Ferryhill and played his entire Town career in the First Division. He scored 96 Ipswich goals and also gained two England caps before becoming a Sunderland legend after joining them in 1985.

FRIDAY 28TH JUNE 1991

Craig Forrest was sent off on his ninth international appearance as Honduras defeated Canada 4-2 in Los Angeles in the CONCACAF Gold Cup. Frank Yallop, also playing, probably did not appreciate Forrest's ill discipline.

TUESDAY 29TH JUNE 1982

A crowd of 75,000 packed Real Madrid's Bernabeu as England, captained by Mick Mills, fought out a dour 0-0 draw with West Germany in the World Cup finals. Terry Butcher and Paul Mariner also played.

TUESDAY 30TH JUNE 1946

Allan Hunter was born in Sion Mills, Northern Ireland. An outstanding centre-back, Hunter amassed 355 Town appearances and won 47 caps for his country whilst at Portman Road. His formidable partnership with Kevin Beattie saw Hunter win Player of the Year in 1975-76.

WEDNESDAY 30TH JUNE 2004

Leeds United signed Greenwich-born midfielder Jermaine Wright on a free transfer. Wright divided the Town fans in his Portman Road spell, which saw him amass 221 games and score some important goals.

IPSWICH TOWN
On This Day

JULY

WEDNESDAY 1st JULY 1953

Ex-Wolverhampton Wanderers and Arsenal striker Alan Sunderland was born in Mexborough. He scored 13 Town goals, many crucial in avoiding relegation in the 1983/84 campaign, and famously netted the winning goal for Arsenal against Manchester United in the 1979 FA Cup Final.

FRIDAY 1st JULY 2005

Castro Sito, able to play in both full-back slots, was signed from Spanish side Racing Ferrol after impressing on trial. Sito returned to Spain after scoring once, gaining two red cards and making 51 starts.

THURSDAY 2nd JULY 1964

Ian Cranson, a rugged and commanding centre-back was born in Easington. Cranson came through the Ipswich Town production line and earned five England under-21 caps in his time at Portman Road, as well as notching 166 appearances for Town over five years.

MONDAY 2nd JULY 2007

Winger Darren Currie joined Luton Town on a free transfer. Luton became Currie's eleventh club in fourteen years after he scored nine goals in Suffolk after signing from Brighton & Hove Albion for £250,000.

SATURDAY 3rd JULY 1926

Alf Ramsey signed Chorley-born goalkeeper Charlie Ashcroft. The Lancastrian won England B honours while with Liverpool before joining Town. A broken arm cut short his career after just 7 appearances.

SUNDAY 3rd JULY 1966

Creative forward Neil Woods was born in York. One of John Duncan's first signings, Woods joined for £120,000 from Rangers, but never settled in Suffolk due to injuries and eventually forged an impressive career with Grimsby Town after 29 appearances and 7 goals at Portman Road.

MONDAY 4th JULY 1988

All-action midfielder Neill Rimmer joined Wigan Athletic on a free transfer. Rimmer scored three goals in 19 league starts at Portman Road after joining from Everton.

FRIDAY 4TH JULY 2008

Town began their pre-season programme with a 5-1 trouncing of a Combined Universities XI at Loughborough. Billy Clarke (2), Jaime Peters, Owen Garvan and David Norris scored.

FRIDAY 5TH JULY 1935

Cockney Andy Nelson, the popular captain of Town's 1961-62 League Championship-winning side, was born in Silvertown. Nelson made 214 appearances without scoring a goal. He later managed Gillingham and Charlton Athletic before emigrating to Spain.

TUESDAY 5TH JULY 1994

Bulgaria beat Mexico on penalties in New York and progressed to the quarter-finals as Town striker Bontcho Guentchev scored the first decisive spot-kick.

MONDAY 6TH JULY 1936

Scottish inside-forward Bobby Bruce was signed from Sheffield Wednesday. He was prolific at Portman Road scoring 23 goals in two Southern League seasons.

THURSDAY 6TH JULY 1995

Phil Morgan, an England youth international goalkeeper, was released and joined home-town Stoke City on a free transfer. Morgan made only one appearance for the Blues in a 2-0 reverse at Leicester City in 1995.

TUESDAY 7TH JULY 1964

Bontcho Guentchev was born in Tchosevo, Bulgaria, and was signed from Sporting Lisbon midway through the 1992/93 season. The lithe and skilful forward was a popular figure at the club, scoring 11 goals in his time at Portman Road. Bontcho represented his country at the 1994 World Cup finals in the United States while a Town player, and helped Bulgaria reach the semi-finals.

TUESDAY 7TH JULY 1998

Fulham signed defender Gus Uhlenbeek on a free transfer. The erratic Dutchman was signed by George Burley from SV Tops for £100,000 and gave solid service over three years at Portman Road.

SATURDAY 8TH JULY 2006

Nicky Forster scored a penalty as Ipswich drew 1-1 with Boston United in a pre-season friendly at York Street. Town fielded an entirely different XI in both halves of the game.

FRIDAY 9TH JULY 2004

Plumstead-born defensive midfielder Kevin Horlock joined the Blues from West Ham United. Horlock left Suffolk for Doncaster Rovers after failing to score in 62 games.

WEDNESDAY 9TH JULY 2008

A young Town outfit brushed aside non-league Bury Town 3-0 in a pre-season friendly at Ram Meadow. Horlock turned out for Bury four years to the day after signing for Ipswich.

MONDAY 10TH JULY 1911

George Rumbold, born in Alton, was a tough-tackling full-back who scored a number of spectacular goals in his 126 games. His six strikes in the 1948/49 season was a then club record for a full-back.

SATURDAY 10TH JULY 1999

Match-winning winger Bobby Petta left Portman Road for Celtic on a free transfer. Petta, unstoppable on his day, scored nine goals for the club and created numerous others.

THURSDAY 11TH JULY 1974

Hermann Hreidarsson, a gigantic Icelandic international defender, was born in Vestmannaeyjar. The popular left-footer was signed from Wimbledon for £4m in 2000 and endeared himself to the Town faithful with a number of rampaging performances in a three-year spell at Portman Road, which saw him score twice in 128 appearances, before switching to Charlton Athletic and then Portsmouth in 2007, where he collected an FA Cup winners' medal in 2008.

FRIDAY 11TH JULY 2008

The Blues won 2-0 at Brentford in a warm-up for the new season. Danny Haynes and new signing Pim Balkestein – the son of Dutch international Luuk – grabbed the goals.

FRIDAY 12TH JULY 2002

Newcastle United signed imposing Town centre-back Titus Bramble for £5m. Bramble eventually joined Wigan Athletic after failing to win over the Geordie faithful. He impressed many at Portman Road with some barnstorming displays and important goals in a three-year spell.

WEDNESDAY 12TH JULY 2006

Jim Magilton's first win as Town boss: a 2-0 friendly win at Galway United. Nicky Forster and Castro Sito netted at a sun-drenched Terryland Park.

WEDNESDAY 13TH JULY 1994

Bontcho Guentchev's magnificent World Cup campaign finished as Italy defeated Bulgaria 2-1 at the semi-final stage in New York.

TUESDAY 13TH JULY 2004

Joe Royle's Town battled out a goalless draw with Randers FC on the first stop of a Danish pre-season tour. The Superliga team were managed by ex-England defender Colin Todd.

FRIDAY 14TH JULY 1939

Inside-forward Frank Treacy was born on the cusp of World War II in Glasgow. Signed from Scottish junior football, Treacy struggled to establish himself and left for St Mirren after scoring five goals in as many years.

TUESDAY 15TH JULY 2003

Town overcame Southend United 4-2 in the pre-season at Roots Hall despite conceding two early goals, which were to serve notice of the defensive struggles ahead that season.

TUESDAY 16TH JULY 2002

Town, recently relegated from the Premiership, lost 1-0 at AaB Aalborg of Denmark in a friendly. Home keeper Jimmy Neilsen, a judge at Denmark's Miss Sunshine competition the next day, didn't have a save to make.

MONDAY 16TH JULY 2007

Edinburgh-born keeper Neil Alexander was signed from Cardiff City on a free transfer by Jim Magilton. The Scot made 31 impressive Town appearances before completing a dream move to Scottish giants Rangers.

MONDAY 17TH JULY 1950

Town appointed a new trainer/coach from Millwall in Jimmy Forsyth. The Scot served under five different Town managers until his retirement in 1971.

THURSDAY 17TH JULY 2003

Big Frenchman Georges Santos was signed from Grimsby Town on a free transfer. He flourished when moved to centre-back and scored his only Blues goal at Cardiff City.

FRIDAY 18TH JULY 2003

Marcus Bent, Darren Bent and Pablo Counago each scored in a 3-1 victory over Swedish hosts Mjallby as Town continued pre-season unbeaten.

FRIDAY 18TH JULY 2008

Jim Magilton signed Colchester United front-runner Kevin Lisbie for £600,000. Hackney-born Lisbie became the first-ever player to leave Layer Road for Portman Road.

THURSDAY 19TH JULY 1984

Stocky Welsh goalkeeper Lewis Price was born in Bournemouth. The promising stopper came through Town's academy and appeared in 68 league games and earned three Welsh caps before leaving for Derby County.

THURSDAY 19TH JULY 2007

Goalscoring central midfielder Tommy Miller signed from Sunderland for a second Portman Road spell. Easington-born Miller has struck 42 times in 177 games for the Blues up to July 2008.

SUNDAY 20TH JULY 1969

Town's 5-1 crushing of Canada's Vancouver Spartans was witnessed by 3,000 fans, who opted to watch the summer friendly instead of the historic first-ever moon landings which were being screened live on TV.

TUESDAY 20TH JULY 2004

Oxford United were hit for five in a friendly at the Kassam Stadium with Jim Magilton scoring in the 90th minute against his old club.

TUESDAY 21st JULY 1953

Brian 'Noddy' Talbot was born in Ipswich. The combative midfielder spent seven seasons in the first team, playing 227 matches and claiming five England caps, before joining Arsenal for £450,000.

MONDAY 21st JULY 2008

Local lad Richard Wright signed from West Ham United for £500,000 to begin a second spell with Town after leaving in 2001, after 291 games.

FRIDAY 22nd JULY 1994

Stowmarket Town were smashed 7-0 as John Lyall's men continued pre-season on fire. Neil Gregory scored a hat-trick but Tony Vaughan was stretchered off with an ankle injury.

TUESDAY 22nd JULY 2003

Swedish outfit Trelleborgs were seen off 5-0 in Town's final game on their pre-season tour. Darren Bent, Pablo Counago, Martijn Reuser, Marcus Bent and Fabian Wilnis each netted as young Irish centre-back Gerard Nash was taken to hospital with a bad eye injury.

SUNDAY 23rd JULY 2000

George Burley's troops continued their pre-season in a winning vein after promotion to the Premiership with a comfortable 2-0 win against Estonia's Flora Tallinn.

SUNDAY 23rd JULY 2000

Mick Stockwell joined Colchester United on a free transfer. He made 146 appearances at Layer Road and scored 24 goals.

SATURDAY 24th JULY 1982

Town defeated Tampa Bay Rowdies 3-1 in a friendly. The Americans featured Rodney Marsh and future Town assistant boss John Gorman in their line-up. Town had signed Tony Kinsella from the Rowdies for £40,000 only a few months before.

WEDNESDAY 24th JULY 2002

The two Darrens – Bent and Ambrose – poached late goals as Bristol Rovers were pipped 2-1 in a friendly at Clevedon.

SUNDAY 25TH JULY 1926

Ken Malcolm was born in Arbroath. The left-back played 293 games for Ipswich before retiring in 1963. He also had the honour of captaining Town in their first-ever European tie.

THURSDAY 25TH JULY 1946

Left-back Colin Harper, born in Ipswich, scored six goals in 180 Town appearances and was a regular in defence under Bobby Robson's stewardship in the early 1970s.

MONDAY 26TH JULY 1931

John Elsworthy, who scored 52 goals in 435 games, was born in Newport. The Welsh wing-half won two Third Division South titles, one Second Division and a First Division title for Town. Elsworthy made the 1958 Wales World Cup finals squad for Sweden, but was omitted at the last moment due to a lack of funds and was never capped by his country.

SUNDAY 26TH JULY 1953

Four Town players were injured returning from a charity cricket match at Gorleston. Their Land Rover, borrowed from John Cobbold, overturned at Yoxford.

WEDNESDAY 27TH JULY 1988

Middlesbrough signed Mark Brennan from Town for £375,000. The gifted midfielder came through Town's youth set-up, won five England under-21 caps and scored 25 goals in 209 games.

WEDNESDAY 27TH JULY 1994

Simon Milton's 21st-minute long-range strike gave Town a 1-0 victory over Finland's FC Jazz as preparations for the season continued. The match was watched by 4,000 fans in blistering heat as temperatures topped 80 degrees.

THURSDAY 28TH JULY 1966

Long-throw expert Andy Legg was born in Neath, Wales. Town signed the Welsh international on loan from Birmingham City in the 1997/98 season and he scored once in six fairly ineffectual games.

MONDAY 28TH JULY 2003

Joe Royle signed goalkeeper Kelvin Davis from Luton Town on a free transfer. Bedford-born Davis was magnificent for two seasons at Portman Road before leaving to join Sunderland for £1,250,000 in 2005.

MONDAY 29TH JULY 1985

Under Bobby Ferguson, Ipswich focused their pre-season campaign against lower league domestic opposition. Mansfield Town were defeated 2-0 at Field Mill with strikes from Trevor Putney and Mich D'Avray.

MONDAY 29TH JULY 2002

Promising Suffolk-born defender Ashley Nicholls left Ipswich after failing to make a single appearance. Nicholls was signed by Darlington on a free transfer and made 73 starts for The Quakers.

SATURDAY 30TH JULY 1966

Sir Alf Ramsey, Ipswich Town manager for eight years, led England to their highest footballing honour as West Germany were defeated 4-2 at Wembley in the World Cup Final.

SATURDAY 30TH JULY 1994

Town completed their Finnish tour with a 100% record thanks to a 4-0 trouncing of Ekenas including a brace from out-of-contract speedster Chris Kiwomya.

SATURDAY 31ST JULY 1920

Stan Parker, a free-scoring forward, was born in Worksop. Parker scored on his league debut against Port Vale in 1946 and tallied 47 career goals at Portman Road over five seasons.

MONDAY 31ST JULY 2006

Promising Ipswich-born striker Jack Ainsley scored on his England under-17 debut as Sweden were overcome 4-2 in the Nordic Tournament in the Faroe Islands.

IPSWICH TOWN
On This Day

AUGUST

MONDAY 1st AUGUST 1938

Dennis Thrower, a popular wing-half who mainly played as cover, was born in Ipswich. He made his debut in August 1956 against Bournemouth & Boscombe Athletic aged 18 years and 28 days – then a record as the youngest player to appear in a Town shirt.

SATURDAY 1st AUGUST 1981

A tremendous attendance of 25,000 at Ibrox saw Town defeat Scottish giants Rangers 2-1 in a challenge match. Glasgow-born John Wark scored both Ipswich goals.

THURSDAY 2nd AUGUST 1984

Bobby Ferguson's men drew 1-1 with Swedish side Norrstrands in pre-season. The 4,000 crowd were treated to a post-match penalty shoot-out which Town won thanks to two Paul Cooper saves.

WEDNESDAY 2nd AUGUST 1989

Mich D'Avray's testimonial game saw a John Duncan-managed Town XI defeated 3-2 by the 1981 Uefa Cup-winning side before 6,000 at Portman Road.

MONDAY 3rd AUGUST 1942

Talented Scottish winger Frank Brogan was born in Glasgow. Signed from Celtic, Brogan was Town's top league scorer when they won the Second Division championship in 1967/68 with 17 goals in 36 games.

SATURDAY 3rd AUGUST 2002

The last of that season's pre-season friendlies saw Celta Vigo defeated 2-1 thanks to two late Darren Ambrose goals after Benni McCarthy had put the Spanish Primera Division side ahead.

SUNDAY 4th AUGUST 1957

Born in Glasgow, John Wark made his Town league debut in March 1975 but it was not until 1976-77 he became a regular in Town's midfield and gave notice of his goalscoring prowess with 10 goals in 33 games. Making his Scotland debut in 1979, Wark won both the FA Cup and Uefa Cup with Ipswich; his contribution was an outstanding 14 goals from midfield. He ended up with 190 goals in 678 games.

SATURDAY 4TH AUGUST 2001

Dutch giants PSV Eindhoven won 2-0 at Portman Road in a warm-up to a woeful Premiership campaign which ended in relegation.

SUNDAY 5TH AUGUST 1934

Wrexham-born wing-half Cyril Lea made 123 appearances for Ipswich and scored two goals. He also won two Welsh caps with Town and was Bobby Robson's assistant when they won the FA Cup Final.

SUNDAY 5TH AUGUST 2007

Spanish penalty-box technician Pablo Counago bagged two as Greek side Panathinaikos went down 2-0 at Portman Road in a friendly.

TUESDAY 6TH AUGUST 1957

Forward John Deehan was born in Solihull, West Midlands. Deehan joined Ipswich from Norwich City in a swap deal with Trevor Putney and scored ten League goals in the 1986/87 season.

SATURDAY 6TH AUGUST 2006

Jim Magilton's first league game as the Town boss ended in defeat as Crystal Palace won 2-1 in Suffolk. Nicky Forster's fine goal gave Ipswich the lead before ex-Blue James Scowcroft netted the Eagles' winner.

MONDAY 7TH AUGUST 1972

Towering centre-half Phil Whelan was born in Stockport. Whelan, signed by John Lyall, headed home on his debut in a crucial 2-1 win over Southend United in the 1991/92 Division Two-winning season. He won an England under-21 cap and was later transferred to Middlesbrough for £300,000.

SATURDAY 7TH AUGUST 1999

Nottingham Forest were beaten 3-1 on the opening day of the season thanks to goals from James Scowcroft, David Johnson and Richard Naylor.

TUESDAY 8TH AUGUST 1950

England goalkeeper Phil Parkes was born in Sedgley and played three games for Town at the end of the 1990/91 season. The QPR and West Ham legend won the FA Cup under John Lyall's leadership with the Hammers in 1980.

MONDAY 8TH AUGUST 1955

Alf Ramsey was appointed Town's third manager after appearing in 250 games for Tottenham Hotspur. He won three titles – Third Division (South), Second Division and First Division – in the space of five years and established Ipswich as a true force. He racked up 176 victories before leading England to World Cup success in 1966.

TUESDAY 9TH AUGUST 2005

South African defender Mark Fish was hauled off at half-time on his debut and never appeared for Town again after a woeful display in a 2-1 defeat at Queens Park Rangers.

MONDAY 9TH AUGUST 1979

Forward Pablo Counago was born in Pontevedra, Spain. The skilful striker was signed by George Burley from Celta Vigo on a free transfer after impressing the Scot playing for Spain under-21s. Back for a second spell at Portman Road, Counago has racked up an impressive 47 goals in 106 starts to July 2008.

SATURDAY 10TH AUGUST 1968

A 1-0 victory over Wolverhampton Wanderers at a packed Portman Road gave Division Two champions Ipswich a great start back in the top flight. John O'Rourke's header was enough to beat future Town custodian Phil Parkes.

SATURDAY 10TH AUGUST 2002

Town started the season in fine style with a 2-0 win at Walsall in front of the Sky cameras with goals from Darren Ambrose and Marcus Bent.

SATURDAY 11TH AUGUST 1962

Town's season started off dreadfully with a 5-1 thrashing by Tottenham Hotspur at Portman Road in the Charity Shield. Roy Stephenson's strike was a mere consolation as the champions were pulled apart by Bill Nicholson's men.

WEDNESDAY 11TH AUGUST 2004

Wallsend-born midfielder Tony Dinning made his Blues loan debut from Wigan Athletic in a 1-1 draw at Nottingham Forest.

SATURDAY 12TH AUGUST 1972

Following an *Evening Star* competition to find a new badge, Town won 2-1 at Old Trafford wearing the Suffolk Punch horse for the first time.

SATURDAY 12TH AUGUST 1979

A dismal performance in the Charity Shield saw Town crushed 5-0 by Nottingham Forest only three months after defeating Arsenal at Wembley.

WEDNESDAY 13TH AUGUST 2003

Dean Bowditch's first Town goal, in extra-time, pipped Kidderminster Harriers 1-0 in the League Cup, in the clubs' first professional meeting.

SATURDAY 13TH AUGUST 2005

Joe Royle's Town fought hard to pick up a point in a goalless Championship encounter at Leicester City. Richard Naylor's early miss from a Kevin Horlock cross spurred the Foxes to a constant bombardment as Welshman Lewis Price made numerous fine saves. Price was replaced due to injury by youngster Shane Supple who lived up to his name with some agile stops.

SATURDAY 14TH AUGUST 1971

The new Portman Road stand was unveiled before a goalless draw with Everton. The stand cost £180,000 – with nearly 3,700 seats – raising the capacity to nearly 37,000 and trimming the pitch width by six feet.

SATURDAY 14TH AUGUST 1993

Bubble-haired forward Ian Marshall scored on his Town debut as the Blues won 3-0 at Oldham Athletic on the opening day of the season. Marshall had joined from the Latics for £750,000 earlier that month.

SATURDAY 15TH AUGUST 1987

The author's first Ipswich game was a 1-1 draw with Aston Villa before 14,580 in Suffolk. Chris O'Donnell's own goal put Villa ahead before Nigel Gleghorn earned John Duncan a point in his first game in charge.

SATURDAY 15TH AUGUST 1992

Exactly five years later, the same two sides met in the first weekend of the newly formed Premiership. Gavin Johnson's quality strike was equalled by former Blue Dalian Atkinson in the second half.

SUNDAY 16TH AUGUST 1908

Oswald Parry, a tough-tackling full-back, was born in Merthyr Tydfil. Parry was an ever-present in Ipswich's first season in the Football League and left Portman Road after making 188 appearances – his last at the age of 40.

SATURDAY 16TH AUGUST 1980

John Wark's header was enough to give Ipswich the win at Filbert Street before 21,460 fans in a Division One clash.

SATURDAY 17TH AUGUST 1991

A 3-3 draw at Bristol Rovers marked the start of Town's championship-winning campaign. Future Town legend Marcus Stewart scored for the Pirates while Dozzell, Goddard and Stockwell netted for Ipswich.

SATURDAY 17TH AUGUST 1968

An impressive 3-1 win at Leicester City saw Ray Crawford score and begin a run of finding the net for seven straight games.

TUESDAY 18TH AUGUST 1970

Before Town's first home match of the season against Coventry City, four freefall parachutists from the Red Devils delivered the match ball to the centre spot after jumping from 7,000 feet. The impressive display had no impact as Town lost 2-0.

SUNDAY 18TH AUGUST 2002

Leicester City were sent spinning 6-1 at Portman Road as the Blues marked their first home game after Premiership relegation with aplomb. Matt Holland (2) and Pablo Counago (2) led the rout.

SATURDAY 18TH AUGUST 2007

Dutch defender Fabian Wilnis became the Blues' most sent-off player as he was dismissed in the 1-1 draw at Plymouth Argyle. It was his fourth dismissal for Town which included three red cards against the Pilgrims.

SATURDAY 19TH AUGUST 1972

Ipswich's first home win of the season was marked with headers from Trevor Whymark and John Miller. Birmingham City keeper Paul Cooper was at fault for both goals in a 2-0 win.

SATURDAY 19TH AUGUST 2006

New loan midfielders Mark Noble and Simon Walton – signed from West Ham United and Charlton Athletic, respectively – made their debuts in a 0-0 draw with Hull City.

SATURDAY 20TH AUGUST 1955

Alf Ramsey's first game as Ipswich manager ended in a surprise 2-0 defeat to Torquay United at Portman Road. Town went on to finish third in Division Three (South) that season.

SATURDAY 20TH AUGUST 1977

Wayne Brown was born in Barking. Powerful in the air, Brown left Town when they signed Hermann Hreidarsson and he ended up at Watford before helping to earn Hull City promotion to the Premiership. Brown made 37 starts and scored once.

SATURDAY 20TH AUGUST 1977

On the same day, Town defeated Arsenal 1-0 at Portman Road in front of a huge attendance of 30,154. David Geddis scored the goal.

SATURDAY 21ST AUGUST 1948

The Blues started off their Division Three (South) campaign with a bang as Bristol Rovers were torn apart 6-1 at Eastville. It was Town's only League victory so far at the Gas in fifteen attempts.

SATURDAY 21ST AUGUST 1993

Town went top of the Premiership with their third successive win. Chelsea were beaten 1-0 at Portman Road thanks to a goal from Ian Marshall.

WEDNESDAY 22ND AUGUST 1928

Creative outside-right James Gaynor was born in Dublin. Town signed him from Shamrock Rovers and Gaynor made 47 league appearances, scoring three goals and setting up many others over two seasons.

TUESDAY 22ND AUGUST 2000

Ipswich made an early impression on the Premiership with a cracking 1-1 home draw versus Manchester United. A fine early goal from Dutch raider Fabian Wilnis set the tone before David Beckham equalised.

FRIDAY 23rd AUGUST 1963

Born in Fulham, Simon Milton made his name at Portman Road with some explosive goals after charging forward from midfield in a career which saw him collect 55 goals in 332 appearances. He turned down a move to Norwich City, while with Town, and was voted supporters' Player of the Year for 1995/96.

TUESDAY 23rd AUGUST 1966

Portman Road celebrated strikes from Eddie Spearritt, Gerard Baker and Frank Brogan as Huddersfield Town were emphatically sent back to Yorkshire with a 3-0 drubbing to ponder.

TUESDAY 24th AUGUST 1976

Town drew 1-1 at Everton in a Division One midweek encounter. A crowd of 33,070 saw Kevin Beattie's goal but it was not enough to give Town a first win at Everton in their twelfth visit.

SATURDAY 24th AUGUST 1963

A 3-1 Portman Road victory over Burnley, capped with goals from Doug Moran and Ray Crawford (2), would be the final time Town tasted victory in 23 games.

THURSDAY 24th AUGUST 1972

Defender Bruce Twamley registered his second Canadian cap in a 1-0 World Cup qualifying defeat to Mexico.

THURSDAY 25th AUGUST 1955

Oswestry-born Les Tibbott won one Wales under-21 cap with Town and racked up 54 league games at Portman Road in three years.

SATURDAY 25th AUGUST 1956

Town legend Tommy Parker made the last of his 465 Ipswich appearances in a 2-0 Division Three (South) home match with Millwall.

SATURDAY 25th AUGUST 1990

John Lyall's first game in charge of the Blues ended in a 2-0 Portman Road defeat to Sheffield Wednesday. Lyall was hired months before when working as technical co-ordinator for Tottenham Hotspur.

SATURDAY 25TH AUGUST 1984

A useful 0-0 draw at Upton Park saw Town kick off the Division One season. Future Town strikers Paul Goddard and Steve Whitton were kept quiet for the East Londoners.

SATURDAY 26TH AUGUST 1967

A good start to the season. A 5-0 hammering of Bristol City included a Frank Brogan hat-trick, and was the first home game of Town's title-winning Division Two campaign.

SATURDAY 26TH AUGUST 1978

The Blues won their first game of the season, comfortably despatching Manchester United 3-0 at Portman Road with a brace from Paul Mariner and a strike from Brian Talbot.

SATURDAY 26TH AUGUST 1995

A 0-0 draw at West Bromwich Albion saw the Blues pick up a first point away from home following ten consecutive away defeats.

SATURDAY 27TH AUGUST 1938

Town's Football League baptism arrived with a 4-2 Portman Road victory over Southend United, who travelled to the game by boat. A crowd of 19,242 witnessed goals from Bryn Davies, Gilbert Alsop and a brace from Fred Jones.

SATURDAY 27TH AUGUST 1977

Ipswich's day turned sour despite claiming a point at Old Trafford in a 0-0 Division One clash. A thief broke into the visitors' dressing room and stole Roger Osborne's false teeth.

SATURDAY 28TH AUGUST 1965

Peckham-born Dave Harper became the first Ipswich player to appear as a substitute. He replaced Frank Brogan in a 2-0 defeat at Charlton Athletic.

SATURDAY 28TH AUGUST 1982

Bobby Ferguson, replacing Town legend Bobby Robson, celebrated his first game as manager with a 1-1 draw at Brighton & Hove Albion in the First Division.

SATURDAY 29TH AUGUST 1936

Town celebrated their first ever match as a professional team with a 4-1 thumping over Tunbridge Wells Rangers in front of 14,211 spectators in the Southern League. George Dobson, Jackie Williams, Bobby Bruce and Jack Blackwell netted.

TUESDAY 29TH AUGUST 1961

Ipswich celebrated their first-ever win in the First Division with a 6-2 thumping of then-mighty Burnley who were to finish runners-up to Town that season. All five Blues forwards found the net.

THURSDAY 29TH AUGUST 2002

Pablo Counago scored Ipswich's first hat-trick against European opposition for 22 years as Town strolled past Luxembourg part-timers Avenir Beggen 8-1 at Portman Road in the Uefa Cup.

SUNDAY 30TH AUGUST 1992

Town drew 1-1 with Tottenham Hotspur at Portman Road in front of the Sky cameras, and 20,100 fans. John Wark's goal was cancelled out by a wind-assisted strike from Spurs defender Jason Cundy from the halfway line.

MONDAY 30TH AUGUST 1999

Barnsley were crushed 6-1 at Portman Road in Division One thanks to a brilliant attacking display. The two teams were to meet in the play-off final later that season.

SUNDAY 31ST AUGUST 1947

Ian Collard, an injury-plagued midfielder, was born in County Durham. Collard retired from Town with a hip complaint after playing 111 games in seven years.

SATURDAY 31ST AUGUST 1996

A frenetic six-goal thriller at Boundary Park saw the spoils shared in Division One. Alex Mathie (2) and Micky Stockwell scored Town's goals as Oldham fans bayed for the sacking of manager Graeme Sharp.

IPSWICH TOWN
On This Day

SEPTEMBER

WEDNESDAY 1st SEPTEMBER 1954

Town, down at half-time, thumped Middlesbrough 6-1 in their first-ever meeting at Portman Road. Tom Garneys (2), Alex Crowe (2), Billy Reed and George McLuckie bagged the goals.

WEDNESDAY 1st SEPTEMBER 1954

Basildon-born Glenn Keeley made four appearances for Town after winning England youth honours whilst at Portman Road. 'Killer' Keeley eventually acquired legendary status at Blackburn Rovers due to his reckless challenges.

SATURDAY 1st SEPTEMBER 1962

Jimmy Leadbetter's first-half strike in a 1-1 draw with Nottingham Forest was the 32nd consecutive game that Town had scored at home.

SATURDAY 2nd SEPTEMBER 1939

Ipswich drew 1-1 with Norwich City in the Third Division (South). It was the last Football League game for six years: war was declared the next day.

SATURDAY 2nd SEPTEMBER 1995

Alex Mathie grabbed a hat-trick as Town kept up their 100% home record by destroying eventual champions Sunderland 3-0.

TUESDAY 3rd SEPTEMBER 1963

Denis Law netted a hat-trick as Division One leaders Manchester United won 7-2 in Suffolk. Scotsman Doug Moran poached both Ipswich goals.

SATURDAY 3rd SEPTEMBER 1977

Town beat Chelsea 1-0 at Portman Road and future Blues legend Russell Osman made his debut. The centre back, who won 11 England caps, went on to score 21 goals in 374 Town appearances and was an ever present in the 1979/80 and 1980/81 seasons. Osman had unsuccessful managerial stints at Bristol City and Cardiff City.

THURSDAY 3rd SEPTEMBER 1981

Escape to Victory premiered in London. Town players John Wark, Russell Osman, Kevin O'Callaghan, Robin Turner and Laurie Sivell starred with Pelé, Michael Caine and Sylvester Stallone. Turner and Sivell were cast as German soldiers. Pelé's overhead kick in the final scene took just one take!

SATURDAY 4TH SEPTEMBER 1954

Hull City's Bob Crosbie scored four times as Town went down 4-2 at Boothferry Park in Division Two. It was to spark a record run of ten consecutive defeats for the Blues.

SATURDAY 4TH SEPTEMBER 1965

Plymouth Argyle were crushed 4-1 in Ipswich's only victory on this day. Bill McGarry's team were mid-table in Division Two following the win.

WEDNESDAY 5TH SEPTEMBER 1951

Brighton & Hove Albion were walloped 5-0 in Division Three (South) in Town's biggest win against the Seagulls. The South Coast side wreaked revenge with a 5-1 victory at the Goldstone Ground a week later.

SATURDAY 5TH SEPTEMBER 1964

The Blues crashed 2-1 at Norwich City. Jackie Milburn resigned as manager after an indifferent 16-month spell.

FRIDAY 5TH SEPTEMBER 1975

Chairman John Cobbold had a narrow escape when a bomb went off at the London Hilton only ten minutes after he had been there drinking coffee. Two people were killed.

SATURDAY 6TH SEPTEMBER 1958

Legendary forward Ray Crawford was signed from Portsmouth for £5,000 and was to etch his name in Ipswich history – helping the club win back-to-back titles: Division Two in 1961 and the League Championship in 1962. In two spells at Town he scored 228 goals in 354 games, won 2 England caps and became the first player to score hat-tricks in the Football League, FA Cup, League Cup and European Cup.

SATURDAY 6TH SEPTEMBER 1969

Norwich-born winger Clive Woods made the first of 338 Blues appearances in a 2-0 victory over Newcastle United at Portman Road. Woods bemused the best of defences with tremendous skill and technique and was voted man-of-the-match in the FA Cup Final win in 1978. In 1980 he joined the small group of players to have played for both Town and their local rivals Norwich City.

SATURDAY 7TH SEPTEMBER 1946

Town's first home league win over Norwich City saw the Blues triumph 5-0. Camberwell-born Albert Day scored a hat-trick on his debut.

TUESDAY 7TH SEPTEMBER 1971

George Best inspired Manchester United to victory in a 3-1 League Cup win over Ipswich. In the second half, a small section of the crowd began chanting for the sacking of Bobby Robson.

SATURDAY 7TH SEPTEMBER 1996

Town crashed 3-1 to Huddersfield Town as Richard Wright was carried off with back spasms on 14 minutes. With no substitute goalkeeper, forward Neil Gregory was beaten three times.

TUESDAY 8TH SEPTEMBER 1964

Jackie Milburn resigned as manager with Town bottom of Division Two as the genial yet ineffective Geordie legend suffered from poor health.

TUESDAY 8TH SEPTEMBER 1998

James Scowcroft's brace in a 3-1 Division One win over Bradford City saw the striker in the middle of a hot streak of six goals in five games.

THURSDAY 9TH SEPTEMBER 1948

England striker Tommy Lawton scored four goals as Notts County destroyed the Blues 9-2 at Meadow Lane in Division Three (South).

WEDNESDAY 9TH SEPTEMBER 1953

Town equalled their biggest victory in the Football League by whipping Gillingham 6-1 at Portman Road in a game which saw five different Ipswich goalscorers.

SATURDAY 10TH SEPTEMBER 1955

Robin Turner was born in Carlisle. The striker showed fine loyalty in his Town career which saw only 22 league starts over nine years.

SATURDAY 10TH SEPTEMBER 1983

Stoke City were crushed 5-0 at Ipswich as Town stayed on the heels of West Ham United at the top of the First Division. John Wark hit a brace.

MONDAY 11TH SEPTEMBER 1961

Ipswich's first cup tie with Manchester City saw Town triumph 4-2 in the League Cup first round in Suffolk. The scoreline exactly reversed the league mauling City inflicted weeks earlier.

SATURDAY 11TH SEPTEMBER 1999

Despite John McGreal's sending off, a late James Scowcroft goal clinched a 1-1 draw and extended an unbeaten run at Portsmouth to 33 years.

TUESDAY 12TH SEPTEMBER 1967

The Blues walloped Southampton 5-2 in the League Cup second round. Scorers Ray Crawford (4) and Frank Brogan delighted the 17,202 fans.

WEDNESDAY 12TH SEPTEMBER 2007

Flame-haired defender Chris Casement scored an own goal but his Northern Ireland under-21 side beat Luxembourg 2-1 in a European Championship qualifier.

SATURDAY 13TH SEPTEMBER 1947

The Blues registered a then-record away victory with a 5-1 thrashing of rivals Norwich. Stan Parker set Town on their way with a goal in the first minute.

SATURDAY 13TH SEPTEMBER 2003

Dublin-born midfielder Alan Mahon made his Town debut in a heavy 4-1 loss at West Bromwich Albion for whom Danish defender Thomas Gaardsoe, previously with Town, scored.

WEDNESDAY 14TH SEPTEMBER 1977

A Swedish pipe band led Town supporters through the town to see the Blues beat Landskrona Bois 1-0 in the first leg of their Uefa Cup first round game in Sweden.

SATURDAY 14TH SEPTEMBER 1996

Richard Naylor made his debut in a 3-1 victory over Sheffield United at Bramall Lane, coming on as a substitute for Alex Mathie. 'Bam Bam' has alternated as both centre-back and centre-forward in an injury blighted Town career and is a firm Portman Road favourite who has given his all in over 300 Town appearances, and counting.

WEDNESDAY 15TH SEPTEMBER 1948

Despite ex-England forward Tommy Lawton's second-half goal at Portman Road, the Blues beat Notts County by the odd goal in five in an enthralling Division Three (South) clash.

WEDNESDAY 15TH SEPTEMBER 1982

A crowd of over 60,000 paid record receipts of 700 million lira (about £300,000) at Rome's Olympic Stadium. AS Roma, inspired by Brazilian Falcão, trounced the Blues 3-0 in the Uefa Cup first round.

FRIDAY 15TH SEPTEMBER 1984

Antonio Murray, a promising midfielder who was a product of Town's fabled academy, was born in Cambridge. Murray was presented his league debut by Joe Royle as a second-half substitute in a 4-1 win at Derby County in the final game of the 2002/03 campaign.

SATURDAY 16TH SEPTEMBER 1972

Rod Belfitt scored a brace and Geoff Hurst, England World Cup-winning hero, was surprisingly sent off for dissent as Town beat Stoke City 2-1 and went second in Division One.

SATURDAY 16TH SEPTEMBER 2000

A superb 2-1 win at Leeds United saw Town continue their excellent start to the Premiership. James Scowcroft and Jermaine Wright got the goals.

WEDNESDAY 17TH SEPTEMBER 1980

Town's first competitive game against Greek opposition saw them run out 5-1 victors against Aris Salonika in an incident-packed Uefa Cup first round clash in front of 20,824 fans. John Wark was the star performer on the night with four goals, of which three were spot-kicks awarded by Portuguese referee Antonio Garrido. He also awarded the incensed visitors a penalty which Palla converted before Paul Mariner's fine finish from a sweeping move completed the scoreline. The result ensured a comfortable cushion to take to an intimidating venue in Greece two weeks later.

TUESDAY 17TH SEPTEMBER 1991

Chris Kiwomya's finish from a brilliantly worked free-kick saw the Blues draw 1-1 at Newcastle United in their Division Two-winning campaign.

TUESDAY 18th SEPTEMBER 1962

Ipswich's first excursion in the European Cup saw them hammer Malta's Floriana 4-1 on a sandy pitch in intense heat. Dynamic front duo Ray Crawford and Ted Phillips each scored twice.

SUNDAY 18th SEPTEMBER 2005

Tempestuous Spanish right-back Castro Sito was sent off for the second time in eight days as Town lost 1-0 to Norwich City at Portman Road in front of 29,184 fans.

SATURDAY 19th SEPTEMBER 1959

Town drubbed Sunderland 6-1 with Dermot Curtis scoring the first three and Ted Phillips the remainder. It's the only time that two Ipswich players have scored a hat-trick in the same league match.

SATURDAY 19th SEPTEMBER 1964

Wing-half John Elsworthy made the last of his 434 Town appearances in a 4-1 stuffing at Portman Road by Bolton Wanderers.

WEDNESDAY 19th SEPTEMBER 1979

Cumbrian-born left-footer Steve McCall made his debut in a 3-1 Uefa Cup victory over Norwegian outfit Skied Oslo. The cultured McCall appeared 331 times – including a run of 166 consecutive games – scoring 12 times. He was capped at England B and under-21 level.

WEDNESDAY 20th SEPTEMBER 1967

Craig Forrest was born in Vancouver. The gangling Canadian shot-stopper played in 312 games for Town and earned 44 caps for his country whilst at Portman Road.

TUESDAY 20th SEPTEMBER 1989

Simon Milton's corking hat-trick saw Town leap to the Division Two summit as they notched their fifth straight league win with a 5-1 thumping of Shrewsbury Town at Gay Meadow.

WEDNESDAY 21st SEPTEMBER 1983

Winger Kevin O'Callaghan played alongside BBC football pundit Mark Lawrenson as the Republic of Ireland crushed Iceland 3-0 in Reykjavik.

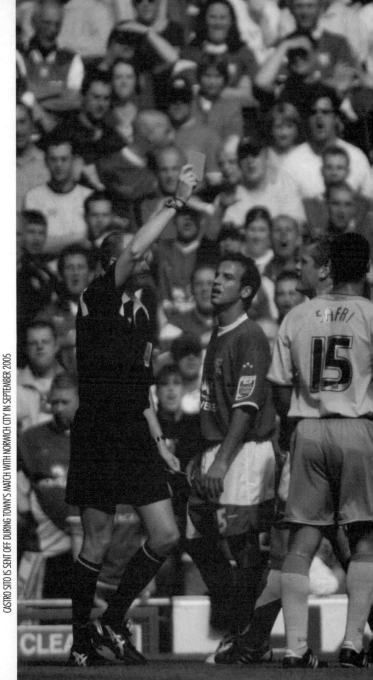

SATURDAY 21st SEPTEMBER 1991

Bristol City were destroyed 4-2 in Suffolk as Town stayed second in Division Two. John Lyall's men put in a tremendous performance capped by Paul Goddard's excellent final goal.

TUESDAY 22nd SEPTEMBER 1999

A 1-1 draw with Crewe Alexandra in the League Cup second round at Portman Road was not enough to see Town through. James Scowcroft's shot ensured a first draw in Suffolk in 30 games.

WEDNESDAY 22nd SEPTEMBER 1954

Billy Reed became the first player to be capped whilst on Town's books. He debuted for Wales in a 3-1 friendly defeat against Yugoslavia at Cardiff.

SATURDAY 22nd SEPTEMBER 1956

Two goals in the first 50 seconds from Wilf Grant and Tom Garneys led Town to a 4-0 home win over Brentford in Division Three (South) at the start of their title-winning season.

WEDNESDAY 22nd SEPTEMBER 1971

Northern Ireland lost 1-0 in Moscow to the USSR in a European Championship qualifier. It marked the first time that two Town players appeared in the same international match – Bryan Hamilton came on as a substitute and Allan Hunter made his Northern Ireland debut.

SATURDAY 23rd SEPTEMBER 1899

Norwich CEYMS were the visitors for the first-ever league match. Henman equalised to gain a 1-1 draw in a Norfolk & Suffolk League encounter.

TUESDAY 23rd SEPTEMBER 1975

Town beat unbeaten Norwich City 2-0 in front of a record crowd for a Portman Road evening match. Goals from Kevin Beattie and Bryan Hamilton were celebrated by 35,077 fans.

MONDAY 24th SEPTEMBER 1956

Ipswich drew at Coventry City 1-1 in their first-ever league match under floodlights. Sheffield-born Doug Millward's goal earned Town their first away point in their Division Three (South)-winning season.

SATURDAY 24TH SEPTEMBER 1994

Despite goals from Eric Cantona and Paul Scholes, Town overcame Manchester United 3-2 at Portman Road thanks to a brace from Liverpool-born midfielder Paul Mason and a Steve Sedgley strike.

TUESDAY 25TH SEPTEMBER 1962

Ipswich crushed Floriana 10-0 at Portman Road in the European Cup preliminary round. Town's biggest European victory saw Ray Crawford become the first Town player to score five goals in a match.

SATURDAY 25TH SEPTEMBER 1982

Town manager Bobby Ferguson won his first match at the seventh attempt as bottom-of-the-table Town crushed Notts County in dramatic style with a 6-0 mauling at Meadow Lane. The win stands as a joint-record away win.

SATURDAY 26TH SEPTEMBER 1964

Under caretaker-manager Jimmy Forsyth, Town recorded their first away win in 30 matches by destroying Middlesbrough 4-2 at Ayresome Park.

SATURDAY 26TH SEPTEMBER 1970

Town went down 2-1 at Chelsea to the 'goal that never was'. Alan Hudson's shot went into the side-netting but amazingly referee Roy Capey signalled a goal despite protests from the Town players.

SATURDAY 26TH SEPTEMBER 1992

Canadian goalkeeper Craig Forrest was sent off after only two minutes at Portman Road as Ipswich drew 0-0 with Sheffield United thanks to a magnificent defensive display.

THURSDAY 27TH SEPTEMBER 2001

Nigerian Finidi George ran riot as Town won 2-1 at Torpedo Moscow to progress to the Uefa Cup second round. George scored and was hauled down for a penalty converted by Marcus Stewart.

SATURDAY 27TH SEPTEMBER 2003

Flying Finn Shefki Kuqi, signed on loan from Sheffield Wednesday the previous day, scored with his first touch as Town picked up their first away win of the season at Watford 2-1. Jim Magilton's exquisite chip sealed the win.

SATURDAY 28TH SEPTEMBER 1946

Albert Day and Geoff Fox grabbed the goals as Town beat Reading 2-0 in Division Three (South).

WEDNESDAY 28TH SEPTEMBER 1977

Sweden's Landskrona Bois were humiliated 5-0 at Portman Road in the Uefa Cup first round, second leg. A crowd of 18,741 saw Trevor Whymark score four goals, the third time he had achieved that feat in an Ipswich shirt.

SUNDAY 29TH SEPTEMBER 1918

Inside-forward Allenby Driver was born in Sheffield. Driver was signed from Norwich City for £3,000 in 1950. He scored on his home debut and scored 25 Town goals in 85 league starts.

WEDNESDAY 29TH SEPTEMBER 1982

Town crushed Roma 3-1 in Suffolk but it was not enough to stop them exiting the Uefa Cup at the first hurdle. A 3-0 reverse in Rome from the first leg was too high a mountain to climb despite goals from Eric Gates, Steve McCall and makeshift striker Terry Butcher.

SATURDAY 29TH SEPTEMBER 1984

The Blues strolled past Aston Villa – who had both Peter Withe and Colin Gibson sent off on 53 minutes by referee David Letts – 3-0 at Portman Road.

SATURDAY 30TH SEPTEMBER 1967

Bustling forward Ron Wigg scored a brace on debut as Town beat Carlisle United 3-1 at Portman Road. Versatile full-back Eddie Spearritt grabbed the other as the Blues remained three points behind leaders Crystal Palace.

WEDNESDAY 30TH SEPTEMBER 1981

Uefa Cup holders Town were dumped out of the competition in the first round. Aberdeen's 3-1 victory at Pittordrie sealed a 4-2 aggregate defeat.

IPSWICH TOWN
On This Day

OCTOBER

MONDAY 1st OCTOBER 1888

At a meeting between the two clubs, Ipswich Association and Ipswich Football Club (actually the rugby club) amalgamated and Ipswich Town Football Club was formed. Oxford blue and white stripes were adopted as the club colours.

SATURDAY 1st OCTOBER 1960

Leeds United, boasting Jack Charlton and Don Revie, were thrashed 5-2 at Elland Road thanks to a Ray Crawford hat-trick as Town marched to the Division Two title.

WEDNESDAY 1st OCTOBER 1980

Eric Gates notched what would be one of the most important goals of his Town career as Ipswich squeaked through to the Uefa Cup second round despite losing 3-1 to Aris Salonika in a white-hot atmosphere in Greece. A seemingly unassailable 5-1 lead from the first leg was whittled down to one goal with 30 minutes to go thanks to strikes from Tsirimokos, Drambis and Zeleliolis before Gates' crisp shot beat Pantziaras on 73 minutes and booked their place in the next round.

WEDNESDAY 2nd OCTOBER 1963

Neil Thompson was born in Beverley, Yorkshire. Thompson, a left-back with a magnificent shot, was signed from Scarborough for £100,000 by John Duncan and he managed 23 goals in a six-year spell in Suffolk.

WEDNESDAY 2nd OCTOBER 1991

David Lowe scored twice as Town beat Bristol Rovers 3-1 in the Full Members' Cup first round. Defender Phil Whelan made his Blues debut.

WEDNESDAY 3rd OCTOBER 1973

In front of 80,000 at the Bernabeu Stadium, Town drew 0-0 with Real Madrid and ensured a safe passage into the Uefa Cup second round. Ipswich's constant attacking shook the Spaniards and their first-leg goal proved enough.

WEDNESDAY 3rd OCTOBER 1979

Norwegian part-timers Skied Oslo were destroyed 7-0 at Portman Road as Town progressed to the Uefa Cup second round 10-1 on aggregate.

SATURDAY 4TH OCTOBER 1890

Reading were defeated 2-0 at Portman Road in Ipswich Town's first ever FA Cup tie. A 'very good' crowd saw George Sherrington and Stanley Turner score the decisive goals.

SATURDAY 4TH OCTOBER 1958

Blues legend Ray Crawford scored the first two of his 227 Town goals in a 4-2 defeat at Swansea Town on his debut. Crawford was the first ever player to score hat-tricks in the Football League, League Cup, FA Cup and European Cup and the first Town player to gain an England cap while on the club's books.

SUNDAY 5TH OCTOBER 1958

Irishman Dermot Curtis became only the second Ipswich player to represent his country as Eire drew 2-2 with Poland in a friendly at Dalymount Park, Dublin.

MONDAY 5TH OCTOBER 1964

Bill McGarry, competitive and uncompromising, was appointed manager of Ipswich and succeeded Jackie Milburn. McGarry led Town to the Second Division championship before later guiding Wolverhampton Wanderers into Europe.

SATURDAY 6TH OCTOBER 1956

Ted Phillips scored his first hat-trick for Town as they conquered high-flying rivals Colchester United 3-1 at Portman Road in Division Three (South).

SATURDAY 6TH OCTOBER 1984

George Burley scored the fastest goal at Newcastle United for over 40 years – his own goal after 20 seconds set Town on their way to a 3-0 drubbing!

SATURDAY 7TH OCTOBER 1950

A 0-0 draw at future Division Three (South) champions Nottingham Forest would be Town's last stalemate for 28 games.

WEDNESDAY 7TH OCTOBER 1987

New left-back Graham Harbey scored his first Blues goal at Northampton Town who were beaten 4-2 in the League Cup second round.

MONDAY 8TH OCTOBER 1956

Dale Roberts, stalwart centre-back and future Ipswich coach, was born in Newcastle. The Geordie joined Atlanta Chiefs after 24 Town appearances before finding success at Hull City. He returned to the club's coaching staff in 1995, but sadly died of cancer in February 2003.

SATURDAY 8TH OCTOBER 1960

A 2-0 Division Two win at the Valley over Charlton Athletic featured hotshot Ted Phillips scoring for the eighth consecutive game.

SATURDAY 8TH OCTOBER 1988

A top-of-the-table Division Two clash in Suffolk saw Town pip Manchester City 1-0 thanks to Jason Dozzell. Skipper David Linighan was dismissed with 18 minutes remaining.

TUESDAY 8TH OCTOBER 2002

A dismal 3-0 defeat at Grimsby Town saw George Burley sacked as manager after an eight-year spell as manager.

SATURDAY 9TH OCTOBER 1965

Town crashed to a surprise 4-3 home loss to Bury. There were seven different goalscorers – Mick McNeil, Gerard Baker and Frank Brogan for Ipswich – and the programme that day cost sixpence.

SATURDAY 9TH OCTOBER 1999

Midfield dynamo Matt Holland's Republic of Ireland debut was a 1-1 European Championship qualifier in Macedonia.

SATURDAY 10TH OCTOBER 1936

Tunbridge Wells Rangers were pipped 2-0 in Kent as the Blues continued their 100% Southern League record. Town's visit to the Garden of England attracted a record crowd of 3,000 for the hosts.

SATURDAY 10TH OCTOBER 1964

Struggling Town fought out a 4-4 draw with third-placed Rotherham United in Suffolk. Scottish striker John Colrain scored twice. The tenacious striker scored 20 career goals at Portman Road before departing for Glentoran.

TUESDAY 11TH OCTOBER 1960

Ipswich's first ever League Cup match saw them produce a dismal display. They were easily beaten by Third Division Barnsley 2-0 at Portman Road.

WEDNESDAY 11TH OCTOBER 1972

Mick Mills won the first of his 42 England caps in a 1-1 draw against Yugoslavia at Wembley witnessed by 50,000 fans.

WEDNESDAY 11TH OCTOBER 1995

Only 1,300 fans, including the author, saw Brescia and Town draw 2-2 in the Anglo-Italian Cup in northern Italy. The host's chairman personally invited Blues fans into the boardroom after the game for a cup of tea after Paul Mason and Steve Sedgley had scored for Ipswich.

WEDNESDAY 12TH OCTOBER 1977

England beat Luxembourg 2-0, in Luxembourg, in a World Cup qualifier. It was the ninth and final cap that Kevin Beattie won for his country while Paul Mariner scored for England.

WEDNESDAY 12TH OCTOBER 1994

Town beat Ipswich Wanderers 7-3 at Humber Doucy Lane to celebrate the opening of the home team's floodlights. Chris Kiwomya scored four goals in front of 600 fans.

SATURDAY 13TH OCTOBER 1928

The Blues defeated Ealing 4-0 in the Southern Amateur League. The game was Town's first appearance at Wembley Stadium, witnessed by 1,200 fans, due to Ealing having to switch venues due to a consistently waterlogged pitch.

SATURDAY 13TH OCTOBER 1973

Town's first-ever win at Stamford Bridge was achieved thanks to goals from David Johnson (2) and Bryan Hamilton in a 3-2 Division One victory.

WEDNESDAY 14TH OCTOBER 1970

Right-back Tommy Carroll scored from the spot on his eighth appearance as Republic of Ireland drew 1-1 with Sweden in a European Championship qualifier in Dublin.

SATURDAY 14TH OCTOBER 1995

Steve Sedgley scored his third goal in three games in a 1-1 draw at Derby County. It would be Town's fifth straight away draw.

TUESDAY 14TH OCTOBER 2003

Ipswich made it six wins in seven games with a 6-1 annihilation of Burnley at Portman Road. Joe Royle's men were up 5-0 at half-time and moved to the edge of the play-off race thanks to a fine display.

SATURDAY 15TH OCTOBER 1898

Claude Woods scored a penalty in Town's 3-1 defeat at Kirkley. However, he also missed one and it was the first spot-kick that Town ever missed.

SATURDAY 15TH OCTOBER 1977

Top-of-the-table Birmingham City, under caretaker-manager Sir Alf Ramsey, were despatched 5-2 at Portman Road in a game which saw referee Alan Turvey leave the pitch after a collision with Eric Gates.

WEDNESDAY 16TH OCTOBER 1878

A group of gentlemen gathered at Ipswich Town Hall on a rainy evening to form a football club. After a lengthy debate, Ipswich Association Football Club was born. A hundred years later the FA Cup would be in the club's trophy room.

TUESDAY 16TH OCTOBER 2007

Billy Clarke, Owen Garvan and Town loanee Mark Noble all played as England under-21s beat Republic of Ireland under-21s 3-0 in Cork.

WEDNESDAY 17TH OCTOBER 1979

Bottom-of-the-table Town had some respite defeating New Zealand 1-0 at Portman Road in a friendly. However, Arnold Muhren picked up a bad injury and was to remain sidelined for months.

TUESDAY 17TH OCTOBER 2006

Winger Gary Roberts, newly signed from Accrington Stanley, made his Town debut in a 3-2 home defeat to Preston North End. His late entry as a substitute for Matt Richards sparked Town into life but not enough for them to claim a point.

SATURDAY 18TH OCTOBER 1947

A Vicarage Road crowd of 9,000 saw Ipswich Town beat Watford 3-2 in Division Three (South) thanks to Stan Parker (2) and Bill Jennings.

SATURDAY 18TH OCTOBER 1986

Geordie Nigel Gleghorn's hat-trick saw Bradford City trumped 4-3 at the Odsal Stadium in Division Two. The Bantams were playing away from Valley Parade due to the shocking fire only a year before.

THURSDAY 19TH OCTOBER 1961

Irish international Kevin O'Callaghan was born in Dagenham. He made 115 top-flight appearances (with 43 from the bench) and was capped 17 times by the Republic of Ireland whilst at Portman Road, appearing in the nation's record victory – 8-0 over Malta in 1983 – and defeat 7-0 at the hands of Brazil a year earlier.

WEDNESDAY 19TH OCTOBER 1977

Spain's Las Palmas were defeated 1-0 thanks to Eric Gates in the Uefa Cup, second round, first leg at Portman Road.

SATURDAY 20TH OCTOBER 1951

Walsall-born winger Joe Ball made his debut in a 3-1 defeat at Crystal Palace. He scored only two Town goals, both against his home-town club.

TUESDAY 20TH OCTOBER 1987

Middlesbrough won 3-1 at Ayresome Park in Division Two. Mich D'Avray scored and Frank Yallop was sent off on 59 minutes.

SATURDAY 21ST OCTOBER 1899

Town registered their first ever victory in league football with a 2-1 victory over Lowestoft Town. Henman and Cotton were the scorers in the Norfolk and Suffolk League clash.

SUNDAY 21ST OCTOBER 2001

A miserable day for Fulham's Portuguese international Luis Boa Morte. He missed a penalty and later in the match was sent off. Jermaine Wright's deserved equaliser for Town ensured a 1-1 Premiership draw at Craven Cottage.

SATURDAY 22ND OCTOBER 1966

In the season's most dramatic match, Ray Crawford notched a hat-trick in a 5-4 home win over Hull City which enabled Ipswich to usurp their opponents at the top of Division Two.

WEDNESDAY 22ND OCTOBER 1980

A glittering second half performance crushed Bohemians Prague 3-0 in the first leg of the second round in the Uefa Cup. John Wark's two second-half goals were added to the four he netted in the first round to take his season's tally to an incredible 14. His deflected shot and smart finish were capped by a fierce free kick from Kevin Beattie from the edge of the box to put Town in a strong position for the return leg.

TUESDAY 23RD OCTOBER 1951

David Johnson, a powerful yet elegant centre-forward who played for both Merseyside clubs as well as Ipswich, was born in Liverpool. Signed from Everton for £200,000, Johnson scored three goals for England whilst at Portman Road, and 46 in his Suffolk spell.

SATURDAY 23RD OCTOBER 1954

A 3-3 Division Two draw at Port Vale ensured Town ended a run of ten straight defeats. George McLuckie, Wilf Grant and Ken Malcolm scored.

WEDNESDAY 24TH OCTOBER 1973

Town embarrassed Lazio 4-0 in a Uefa Cup second round tie with Trevor Whymark scoring all four. The speed and variety of Ipswich's attacks bamboozled the Romans who resorted to vicious tackling which saw David Johnson stretchered off.

SATURDAY 24TH OCTOBER 1998

A brilliant chip from Kieron Dyer sent Ipswich fourth in Division One at rain-lashed Stockport County. Dyer was sent galloping through by loan signing Jonathan Hunt and provided a smart finish.

SATURDAY 25TH OCTOBER 1957

Eventual Division Three (South) champions Queens Park Rangers were defeated 1-0 in Suffolk thanks to a goal from Town's Norwich-born Bill Jennings.

THURSDAY 25TH OCTOBER 1962

Ipswich boss Alf Ramsey received the ultimate honour when appointed as England manager in succession to Walter Winterbottom. Ramsey had won three league titles for the Blues and was later to win the World Cup for his country in 1966.

THURSDAY 25TH OCTOBER 1979

Arsenal goalkeeper Pat Jennings' sister Mari was the Aer Lingus stewardess for Town as they flew back from Zurich after drawing 0-0 with Grasshoppers in the Uefa Cup second round first leg.

THURSDAY 26TH OCTOBER 1950

Bobby Bell, born on this day in Cambridge, was a centre-back signed by Bill McGarry as back-up for Town legend Bill Baxter. Bell, who played 37 games for Ipswich, never really established himself at Portman Road and had the dubious honour of being Norwich City's first loan signing.

TUESDAY 26TH OCTOBER 1982

Full-back Mick Mills made his farewell 741st appearance in Town colours as the Blues crashed out of the League Cup second round 4-1 on aggregate at Liverpool.

WEDNESDAY 27TH OCTOBER 1971

Forward Mick Hill made his Wales debut as his countrymen went down 2-0 in Prague to Czechoslovakia. Hill was one of Bobby Robson's first signings when he joined from Sheffield United for £33,000 in 1969. Robson had earlier tried to sign Hill when manager of Fulham but his £60,000 bid was turned down.

TUESDAY 27TH OCTOBER 1992

Neil Thompson's wonderful free-kick put Town into the hat for the League Cup fourth round as they triumphed 1-0 at Portsmouth in the clubs' only League Cup encounter to date.

SATURDAY 28TH OCTOBER 1995

A magnificent display destroyed Division One Reading 4-1 at Elm Park. Geraint Williams, Gus Uhlenbeek, Alex Mathie and Paul Mason bagged the goals.

TUESDAY 28TH OCTOBER 1997

Matt Holland's 34th minute goal at Birmingham City sparked the first airing of 'One-Nil to the Tractor Boys' as Town fans responded to earlier gloating from their Midlands hosts about a lack of noise.

MONDAY 28TH OCTOBER 2002

Former Everton and Oldham Athletic icon Joe Royle was appointed George Burley's replacement. Royle's Suffolk tenure saw him lose twice in the play-offs before leaving Portman Road after presiding over the lowest league finish in 40 years.

SATURDAY 29TH OCTOBER 1955

Ron Blackman scored on his Blues debut as Reading were hammered 5-1 at Elm Park in a Division Three (South) fixture.

SATURDAY 30TH OCTOBER 1926

Barclays Bank beat Town 3-1 at Portman Road, but the game was held up when rats had to be chased away from the grandstand. Groundsman Walter Woolard's sheep and goats, housed there, were the probable cause.

SATURDAY 30TH OCTOBER 1954

Town crushed Doncaster Rovers 5-1 at Portman Road. Leyton-born Tom Garneys – with four goals – became the first Ipswich player to score more than three in a Football League match. He ignored doctor's advice not to play.

SATURDAY 30TH OCTOBER 1982

High-flying West Bromwich Albion were seen off 6-1 at Portman Road as Town ran riot before 20,011 fans. John Wark scored four, alongside goals from Frans Thijssen and Eric Gates. Romeo Zondervan played for the Baggies.

SATURDAY 31ST OCTOBER 1936

An 11-0 thumping of Cromer Town in the FA Cup divisional final stands as Town's biggest victory to date since turning professional. Five different players scored twice.

FRIDAY 31ST OCTOBER 1969

Hours before a 1-1 draw with Manchester City, vandals broke into Portman Road, damaging two turnstiles and tearing down goal nets.

IPSWICH TOWN
On This Day

NOVEMBER

WEDNESDAY 1st NOVEMBER 1978

Paul Mariner was sent off for the first time in a Town shirt as George Burley's extra-time equaliser at SW Innsbruck in Austria ensured progress to the Cup Winners' Cup third round.

SATURDAY 1st NOVEMBER 1980

West Bromwich Albion could only draw 0-0 at Portman Road despite Russell Osman replacing injured keeper Paul Cooper for the last 40 minutes.

WEDNESDAY 1st NOVEMBER 2000

A first win at Highbury in 21 years saw a weakened Arsenal defeated 2-1 in a League Cup second round clash. Jamie Scowcroft's late winner extended Town's unbeaten run to seven games.

SATURDAY 2nd NOVEMBER 1935

Jock Henderson became the first Town keeper to be sent off as the Blues lost 2-0 at Yarmouth Town. He was shown his marching orders for retaliation.

SATURDAY 2nd NOVEMBER 1991

Goals from John Wark and Gavin Johnson in a 2-2 draw at Leicester City resulted in a sixth consecutive draw for John Lyall's troops.

SATURDAY 3rd NOVEMBER 1962

Manchester United's Scottish international Denis Law scored four times as the Red Devils won 5-3 at Portman Road against the league champions.

SATURDAY 3rd NOVEMBER 1956

Ted Phillips (3) and Tom Garneys ensured Queens Park Rangers were thumped 4-0 at Portman Road in Division Three (South).

SATURDAY 4th NOVEMBER 1922

Ipswich, leaders of the Southern League, slipped to a 3-1 defeat at home to Tufnell Park in a friendly at Portman Road.

SUNDAY 4th NOVEMBER 2007

Norwich City's Darren Huckerby became the 100th opposing player to be sent off against Ipswich in a pulsating 2-2 draw at Carrow Road, where a fine attacking display in the first half was not enough to secure victory.

SATURDAY 5TH NOVEMBER 1966

Ipswich stayed top of Division Two with a 6-1 beating of Northampton Town thanks to Frank Brogan's hat-trick. Ray Crawford, Gerard Baker and future Blues assistant manager Charlie Woods also scored.

WEDNESDAY 5TH NOVEMBER 1980

Ipswich won through to the Uefa Cup third round 3-2, on aggregate, as they hung on in Prague against ferocious Czechoslovakian hosts Bohemians. Town's colossus on a freezing night was Kevin Beattie whose magnificent performance – in only his third game of the season – saw Town home.

SATURDAY 6TH NOVEMBER 1897

Tom Hayward received the dubious honour of becoming the first Town player to be sent off when the Blues lost 3-1 at Framlingham College. Play become 'vigorous' in the later stages and Hayward saw red for a tackle on Reverend H M Mills.

MONDAY 6TH NOVEMBER 1911

A fierce gale saw the roof of the stand at Portman Road blown off. It was replaced for the sum of £60.

SATURDAY 6TH NOVEMBER 1976

Town moved to second place in the First Division table as they turned on the style and hammered West Bromwich Albion 7-0 in front of 25,373 fans as Trevor Whymark scored four. Kevin Beattie, John Wark and Paul Mariner also netted.

SATURDAY 7TH NOVEMBER 1964

Town crushed Portsmouth 7-0 in Division Two thanks to a hat-trick by Frank Brogan and a brace from Danny Hegan. Joe Broadfoot and Gerard Baker also netted.

WEDNESDAY 7TH NOVEMBER 1984

A marvellous 2-1 win at Newcastle United saw Ipswich move into the League Cup fourth round. Mich D'Avray and Eric Gates scored in a game officiated by Keith Hackett – who later became general manager of the Professional Game Match Officials Board.

SATURDAY 8TH NOVEMBER 1953

Town drew 1-1 with Gillingham in Suffolk. Following an interruption when a dog ran on to the pitch, the subsequent dropped ball led to the Gills equaliser from Ken Lambert.

SATURDAY 8TH NOVEMBER 1980

Terry Butcher saw red for the only time in his Ipswich career, thanks mainly to the persistence of Southampton's Kevin Keegan, as Ipswich drew 3-3 in a thriller at The Dell.

SATURDAY 9TH NOVEMBER 1968

Future Town boss Joe Royle headed home twice as title-chasing Everton drew 2-2 in Suffolk in a pulsating Division One encounter, although Town were unlucky not to break the Toffees' 15-game unbeaten record.

WEDNESDAY 9TH NOVEMBER 1983

Mark Brennan made his debut as a brace from John Wark helped the Blues beat Queens Park Rangers 3-2 in the League Cup third round.

WEDNESDAY 10TH NOVEMBER 1937

Town appointed Scott Duncan as their second professional manager. The butcher's son was to be the Blues' first Football League boss. He lasted 18 years in the Portman Road hot-seat and won the Third Division (South) championship in 1955, Town's first ever league honour.

SATURDAY 10TH NOVEMBER 2007

Burly attacker Jonathan Walters scored a hat-trick as Ipswich thrashed high-flying Bristol City 6-0 at Portman Road. David Wright, Tommy Miller (pen) and Pablo Counago added the others.

SATURDAY 11TH NOVEMBER 1967

Goals from Frank Brogan and Eddie Spearritt enable the Blues to fight back against Aston Villa and win 2-1 at Portman Road in Division Two.

SATURDAY 11TH NOVEMBER 1989

An own goal from David May, and a John Wark finish, saw Town pick up a creditable 2-2 draw at Blackburn Rovers. The Blues were still left searching for their first league win at Ewood Park in 23 years.

SATURDAY 12th NOVEMBER 1938

Pat Curran marked his 21st birthday with a goal as Port Vale were beaten 2-0 at Portman Road in the clubs' first-ever encounter. Curran was later to sign for Watford at Sunderland station after being tracked down by Hornets boss Bill Findlay.

SATURDAY 12th NOVEMBER 1977

Brian Talbot's goal was not enough as the Blues were beaten 2-1 at Leicester City in Division One.

SATURDAY 13th NOVEMBER 1937

New Ipswich manager Scott Duncan marked his first game in charge with a 3-0 FA Cup qualifying victory at Chelmsford's Hoffman Athletic.

TUESDAY 13th NOVEMBER 1979

Bobby Robson's testimonial against an England XI saw George Best turn out in an Ipswich shirt before 23,284 Portman Road fans in a 2-2 draw.

SUNDAY 14th NOVEMBER 1976

In front of a 24,000 Celtic Park crowd, goals from Whymark and Mariner saw Ipswich beat Jock Stein's Celtic 2-1 in a friendly.

THURSDAY 14th NOVEMBER 2002

Nigerian Finidi George made his final appearance in a 1-0 defeat at Slovan Liberec which saw Ipswich dumped out of the Uefa Cup second round.

SATURDAY 15th NOVEMBER 1902

The first ever tussle on record between Ipswich Town and Norwich City took place at Norwich with the hosts recording a 1-0 victory.

SATURDAY 15th NOVEMBER 1952

Jack Parry, making his comeback from a broken wrist suffered earlier in the season, was injured again in a 3-1 victory at Walsall. A dislocated thumb saw him replaced by winger James Gaynor.

SATURDAY 15th NOVEMBER 1997

Signed from Bury two days before for £1m, stocky striker David Johnson scored on his debut as Town claimed a 1-1 draw at Wolves.

SATURDAY 16TH NOVEMBER 1957

Ipswich beat table-toppers Liverpool 3-1 at Portman Road roared on by a crowd of 20,591. The Reds hadn't let in a goal in their previous six matches.

WEDNESDAY 16TH NOVEMBER 2005

Midfielder Gavin Williams, signed six days before on loan from West Ham United, appeared as a Wales substitute in a 1-0 friendly defeat to Cyprus.

SATURDAY 17TH NOVEMBER 1894

In a 1-0 win at Colchester Town, Ipswich's Stanley Turner's shot cleared the stand and landed on a horse ploughing a nearby field. The horse bolted and ploughed the fastest, if not the straightest, furrow on record.

SATURDAY 17TH NOVEMBER 1973

Liverpool's Kevin Keegan scored a hat-trick as Town were beaten 4-2 at Anfield in front of watching Prince Harald of Norway and 37,419 others.

SATURDAY 17TH NOVEMBER 1984

A 3-0 home defeat to Tottenham Hotspur was watched by special guest the Governor of Bermuda, Viscount John Dunrossil with music at half-time provided by the Bermuda Regiment.

WEDNESDAY 18TH NOVEMBER 1891

Town's first match against foreign opposition saw a surprising defeat to Canadian/American tourists 2-1 at Portman Road. Ipswich had to offer their visitors £20 to play the fixture, the 35th match of a very long tour.

WEDNESDAY 18TH NOVEMBER 1981

Paul Mariner scored the only goal to clinch England's place at the 1982 World Cup finals. Hungary were beaten in front of 92,000 Wembley fans.

TUESDAY 19TH NOVEMBER 1975

Moustached striker David Johnson scored twice as England under-23s won 3-2 in Lisbon against Portugal.

SUNDAY 19TH NOVEMBER 2006

Danny Haynes came off the bench to score two late goals as Ipswich beat Norwich 3-1. It was Town's first home win against City in eight years.

SATURDAY 20TH NOVEMBER 1948

Bill Jennings scored twice as Exeter City were beaten 3-1 away. It was Ipswich's first win at St James' Park in four attempts.

TUESDAY 20TH NOVEMBER 2007

Jonathan Walters, recently signed from Chester City, won a Republic of Ireland B cap in a 1-1 draw with Scotland.

SATURDAY 21ST NOVEMBER 1925

George Harris scored from the spot in a 3-1 Southern Amateur League win over Aquarius. It was the first time that a Town goalkeeper has scored in a competitive match.

WEDNESDAY 21ST NOVEMBER 1979

Holland beat East Germany 3-2 in a European Championship qualifier and Frans Thijssen scored.

WEDNESDAY 22ND NOVEMBER 1961

Ray Crawford became the first Ipswich player to gain an England cap in a 1-1 draw with Northern Ireland at Wembley. His pass allowed Bobby Charlton to score England's goal.

FRIDAY 22ND NOVEMBER 1963

Tony Mowbray was born in Saltburn. The dominating centre-back helped Town achieve promotion to the Premiership, scoring a vital header in the Play-Off Final against Barnsley at Wembley. He also acted as assistant manager after the Blues sacked George Burley, before moving into management with Hibernian and West Bromwich Albion.

WEDNESDAY 23RD NOVEMBER 1892

Royal Arsenal, soon to be elected to the Football League, visited Portman Road and easily won 5-0. Their inside-left Elliot became the first man to be sent off at Portman Road after being cautioned twice for holding.

SATURDAY 23RD NOVEMBER 1968

A half-time rocket from departing boss Bill McGarry fired up Town and inspired a fight back, which saw the team salvage a 2-2 draw with West Ham United in a Division One clash at Portman Road.

TUESDAY 23RD NOVEMBER 1976

George Burley scored the first of his 11 Town goals in a 3-1 drubbing of Sunderland. Burley, who was to make exactly 500 appearances for Ipswich, was an adventurous defender who successfully marked George Best on his Town debut at Old Trafford as a 17-year-old. He later managed Town to a fifth-place finish in the Premiership and became Scotland manager in January 2008.

WEDNESDAY 23RD NOVEMBER 1977

Town crushed Spanish giants Barcelona 3-0 at Portman Road in the Uefa Cup third round first leg. Johan Cruyff hardly got a kick as the Blues built up a hefty lead through Gates, Whymark and Talbot on one of the greatest nights in Town's history.

SATURDAY 24TH NOVEMBER 1945

Wisbech Town were crushed 5-0 thanks to a Tommy Parker hat-trick in the FA Cup first round, second leg. An FA initiative meant that games would be over two legs to raise funds for clubs after the war.

SATURDAY 24TH NOVEMBER 1984

Two goals for John Wark, recently signed by Liverpool after an illustrious Suffolk spell, saw Town crash 2-0 at Anfield in Division One. Wark would go on to win the league championship with his new employers.

THURSDAY 25TH NOVEMBER 1937

Ken Hancock, Town's goalkeeper when they won the Second Division title in 1967/68, was born in Hampshire. Hancock was signed from Port Vale for £10,000 and played in 108 consecutive games whilst in Suffolk.

SATURDAY 25TH NOVEMBER 1972

The lights literally went out on Town as a Division One encounter with Coventry City was abandoned after 62 minutes due to floodlight failure with the game goalless.

SATURDAY 26TH NOVEMBER 1938

Manchester-born Fred Chadwick grabbed a quartet of goals as Town steamrollered Somerset-based Street 7-0 in the FA Cup first round. Chadwick's goals were added to by Bryn Davies (2) and Charlie Fletcher.

WEDNESDAY 26TH NOVEMBER 1980

A scintillating attacking show saw the Blues overwhelm Widzew Lodz 5-0 at Portman Road and all but confirmed Town's spot in the quarter-finals of the Uefa Cup. An absorbing encounter was crowned by a brilliant hat-trick by midfield king John Wark, which was his second of the competition. It took his European tally in the season to eight goals (all at home). Alan Brazil's ferocious finish, and Paul Mariner's header, completed the scoreline as Ipswich bullied their visitors to the final whistle.

TUESDAY 26TH NOVEMBER 1985

Top-flight Ipswich Town hammered Division Four Swindon Town 6-1 in the League Cup fourth round – their biggest win in the competition.

SATURDAY 27TH NOVEMBER 1971

Sheffield United – inspired by four-goal Alan Woodward – demolished Town 7-0 at Bramall Lane. The result was to begin a run for Bobby Robson's men where they failed to find the target for five successive games. A healthy crowd of 26,233 were in attendance in the Steel City.

SATURDAY 27TH NOVEMBER 1999

Derry-born Sean Friars, signed from Liverpool, made his only appearance as sub for Mick Stockwell in a 2-1 home win over Crewe Alexandra.

WEDNESDAY 28TH NOVEMBER 1962

Ray Crawford and Bobby Blackwood hit the target as Ipswich beat AC Milan 2-1 at Portman Road in the European Cup but it was not enough to reverse the 3-0 first leg defeat from the San Siro. Town struck the woodwork three times. The Italians would go on to lift the trophy.

SATURDAY 28TH NOVEMBER 1981

A 2-0 Division One victory over Manchester City would trigger a record run of nine consecutive victories for Town.

SATURDAY 28TH NOVEMBER 1998

Bustling striker James Scowcroft scored Town's first hat-trick away from Portman Road in a decade as Crewe Alexandra were soundly beaten 3-0. Scowcroft scored 55 goals in 256 Town appearances before joining Leicester City.

SATURDAY 29TH NOVEMBER 2003

Town moved to fourth in Division One with a battling 3-2 win at Cardiff City. Hulking French defender Georges Santos headed his only Blues goal as the Welsh side suffered their second home defeat of the season.

WEDNESDAY 29TH NOVEMBER 2006

Leading at the break thanks to a Gary Roberts long-range strike, Town fell 2-1 at Derby County as loanee Simon Walton was dismissed for a late lunge. Arturo Lupoli headed the Rams' winner in injury-time.

SATURDAY 30TH NOVEMBER 1985

South-African striker Mich D'Avray scored his first Portman Road brace as high-flying Sheffield Wednesday were sent packing 2-1. In total, D'Avray scored 45 goals in 255 games and won a couple of England under-21 caps while at Ipswich.

SATURDAY 30TH NOVEMBER 2002

Jamaican David Johnson scored a brace against his old club as Nottingham Forest stayed third in Division One with a 2-1 victory over Town at the City Ground. A last-minute Gareth Williams own-goal couldn't save the Blues.

IPSWICH TOWN
On This Day

DECEMBER

SATURDAY 1st DECEMBER 1990

Two goals from England striker Steve Bull at Molineux were not enough to see off Town who bagged an excellent 2-2 draw.

SATURDAY 1st DECEMBER 2007

A fine display by Barnsley's German custodian Heinz Muller saw Jim Magilton's Blues held to a 0-0 at Portman Road.

SATURDAY 2nd DECEMBER 1950

A coachload of Swansea City fans wearing Town colours saw the Blues defeat Newport County 2-1. They had come to pay homage to ex-Swans Jim Feeney and Sam McCrory. The players travelled back to Swansea with the fans after the match.

TUESDAY 2nd DECEMBER 1997

A last-minute goal from David Johnson claimed a point against high-flying Middlesbrough at Portman Road in Division One. James Scowcroft earlier saw red in a match which was also significant for Micky Stockwell's 500th appearance for the club.

SATURDAY 3rd DECEMBER 1966

Town remained top of Division Two as Bury were beaten 2-0 in Suffolk thanks to goals from Gerard Baker and Ray Crawford.

SATURDAY 3rd DECEMBER 1994

Manchester City's 2-1 victory at Portman Road kept Town bottom of the Premiership. Subsequent supporter pressure saw manager John Lyall resign after a four-year spell.

SATURDAY 4th DECEMBER 1971

Dutch signing Marco Holster did not work out as well as some of his fellow countrymen. The winger returned to his home country after just 12 appearances in the 1998/99 season.

SATURDAY 4th DECEMBER 1976

England striker Paul Mariner got the goal which saw Liverpool defeated 1-0 as the top two sides in Division One met at Portman Road. A record home league crowd of 35,109 were in attendance.

SATURDAY 5TH DECEMBER 1987

Leaders Bradford City were trounced 4-0 in Suffolk as the Blues backed up a live airing on live BBC national radio with a consummate display. Surinam legend Romeo Zondervan scored twice.

SATURDAY 5TH DECEMBER 1992

Town's 2-2 draw at Coventry City featured a debut from Macedonian defender Vlado Bozinoski – who was recommended to John Lyall by Bobby Robson. He left five months later after making only nine appearances.

SATURDAY 6TH DECEMBER 1924

Willie Havenga, Town's first overseas player, was born in Bloemfontein, South Africa. He made two goals on his debut against Torquay United in 1952 and scored three goals in 19 league games.

SUNDAY 6TH DECEMBER 1992

Town stalwart Frank Yallop won his 14th Canadian cap in a 0-0 draw with Bermuda in Hamilton.

SUNDAY 7TH DECEMBER 1975

Initially signed from Tottenham Hotspur on loan, Jamie Clapham was born in Lincoln. Supporters' Player of the Year in 1998/99, the marauding left-footer appeared in 252 games for Town before joining Birmingham City for £1 million.

WEDNESDAY 7TH DECEMBER 1977

Despite a 3-0 first leg lead, Town lost to Barcelona in a penalty shoot-out at the Nou Camp to the Cruyff-inspired Catalans and crashed out of the Uefa Cup in the third round.

SATURDAY 8TH DECEMBER 1900

An unidentified was the first person arrested at Portman Road, after an opposing player was struck at the end of a 1-0 defeat against King's Lynn.

SATURDAY 8TH DECEMBER 1979

Ferryhill-born Eric Gates scored his first hat-trick for the club in a 4-0 thumping of Manchester City at Portman Road. The diminutive striker scored a total of 96 goals in 378 first-team outings before joining Sunderland.

SATURDAY 9TH DECEMBER 1961

Newly-promoted Ipswich were thumped 3-0 at Aston Villa in a shock defeat before 31,924 spectators. Town recovered to beat the same opposition to claim the Division One title at the end of the season.

SATURDAY 9TH DECEMBER 1972

Town stayed close to the leaders as Crystal Palace were seen off 2-1 at Portman Road thanks to a brace from England striker David Johnson.

WEDNESDAY 10TH DECEMBER 1952

Ipswich destroyed Bradford City 5-1 in an FA Cup second round replay in Suffolk. City featured future England and Somerset cricket captain Brian Close in their ranks who had made his test debut against New Zealand three years earlier.

WEDNESDAY 10TH DECEMBER 1980

In icy and dangerous conditions, which manager Bobby Robson described as 'downright dangerous', Town slalomed into the quarter finals of the Uefa Cup despite losing on the night against Widzew Lodz. With constant snow falling, and most of the outfield players in tracksuit bottoms and gloves with pitch lines marked in orange, Pieta's 55th minute strike was the only goal of the night. Town were elated to progress with no injuries against a team who had earlier knocked out Juventus and Manchester United.

SATURDAY 11TH DECEMBER 1976

Town, on a run of 13 unbeaten games, were 1-0 down at St James' Park. The game with Newcastle United was abandoned at half-time due to a frozen pitch. The replayed Division One game saw John Wark earn a point for the Blues.

SATURDAY 11TH DECEMBER 2004

Former QPR mascot Darren Currie scored on his Blues debut as Town defeated the Hoops 4-2 at Loftus Road.

WEDNESDAY 12TH DECEMBER 1973

Town moved into the Uefa Cup quarter-finals with a 3-1 aggregate win over Twente Enschede in Holland. Bryan Hamilton and Peter Morris scored the crucial goals in a 2-1 victory before 18,000.

DARREN CURRIE SCORES ON HIS TOWN DEBUT AT QPR IN DECEMBER 2004

SATURDAY 12TH DECEMBER 1992

Bontcho Guentchev made his debut in a 3-1 home win over Manchester City. Mick Stockwell, Gavin Johnson and Paul Goddard scored.

WEDNESDAY 13TH DECEMBER 1995

Salernitana, lying sixth in Serie B, were defeated 2-0 in the Anglo-Italian Cup before a small crowd of 6,429 at Portman Road. Tony Mowbray and Neil Gregory made the score sheet.

SATURDAY 13TH DECEMBER 2003

A resolute performance bagged a 0-0 draw at Millwall after Georges Santos was harshly sent off on 59 minutes. Dutchman Fabian Wilnis headed off the line in the dying stages to preserve a six-game unbeaten run.

SATURDAY 14TH DECEMBER 1957

Bobby Johnstone scored in a 2-0 home win over Doncaster Rovers. Johnstone later moved to Canada but failed in a bid to become a singer.

SATURDAY 14TH DECEMBER 1963

Jackie Milburn's men remained rooted to the bottom of Division One as they suffered a 3-1 reverse at Burnley.

SATURDAY 15TH DECEMBER 1956

Ipswich scored their then biggest victory in the Football League by pulverising second-placed Torquay United 6-0 at Portman Road. It was a result that kick-started their march to the championship.

TUESDAY 15TH DECEMBER 1981

Alan Brazil's strike in a 3-2 League Cup fourth round win at Everton sparked a run of him scoring in six straight games.

WEDNESDAY 16TH DECEMBER 1953

Motherwell-born Alex Crowe's 86th minute winner was enough to see off plucky Walthamstow Avenue in an FA Cup second round replay.

SATURDAY 16TH DECEMBER 2006

A fierce shot from Gavin Williams saw off Leeds United – who had Kevin Nicholls sent off for two bookable offences – at Portman Road.

SUNDAY 17TH DECEMBER 1944

Cultured winger Jimmy Robertson was born in Glasgow. Robertson scored in the 1967 FA Cup Final for Tottenham Hotspur and was signed from Arsenal for £50,000 in 1970. He went on to score 12 goals in 98 league and cup games for Ipswich. Robertson also won one cap for Scotland and played for Stoke City, Walsall and Crewe Alexandra.

WEDNESDAY 18TH DECEMBER 1974

George Burley picked up his first representative honours for Scotland in a 3-0 under-23 defeat to England in Aberdeen.

SATURDAY 18TH DECEMBER 1983

A magnificent injury-time own goal from current Bolton Wanderers boss Gary Megson enabled Town to beat Norwich City 2-1 at Portman Road. John Wark's early penalty was equalised by Mark Bowen.

FRIDAY 19TH DECEMBER 1986

Mark Brennan's second brace in six days deflated Plymouth Argyle. Town moved to third after the 2-0 victory.

TUESDAY 19TH DECEMBER 2000

A marvellous extra-time goal from Mark Venus sent the Blues into the League Cup quarter-finals as they won 2-1 at Joe Royle's Manchester City.

FRIDAY 20TH DECEMBER 1963

At last! A 3-2 win over West Ham United at Portman Road, thanks to finishes from Doug Moran, Bobby Blackwood and Gerard Baker, was Ipswich's first victory in 23 games.

FRIDAY 20TH DECEMBER 1968

Alex Mathie, a supremely talented striker, was born in Bathgate. Mathie will be remembered for a magnificent first-half hat-trick against Norwich City in 1998. He scored 47 goals in 108 Ipswich starts.

SATURDAY 20TH DECEMBER 1980

A tremendous 3-1 victory at St Andrew's over Birmingham City kept Town third in the First Division and was the start of an excellent sequence of 20 consecutive undefeated games in the top flight of English football.

SATURDAY 21st DECEMBER 1957

A 2-1 Division Three (South) win over Blackburn Rovers in Suffolk was notable for Tom Garneys' eighth goal in consecutive games – a Town record.

SATURDAY 21st DECEMBER 1968

Town were defeated by Nottingham Forest 3-2, a game watched by Bobby Robson who was scouting for Chelsea at the time. According to Robson – not long after he was appointed Ipswich manager – Cyril Lea, Town's caretaker-manager, gave him a 'very old-fashioned look' at the end of the game.

SATURDAY 22nd DECEMBER 1973

A brilliant brace from Mick Lambert and full-back Geoff Hammond's final Blues goal saw off Birmingham City 3-0 at Portman Road.

SATURDAY 22nd DECEMBER 2001

A splendid first away victory of the season at Tottenham Hotspur was achieved thanks to an overhead kick from Nigerian Finidi George and Alun Armstrong's 88th minute winner. Teddy Sheringham was sent off for Spurs as Town stayed bottom of the Premier League.

SATURDAY 23rd DECEMBER 1893

Fred Turner claimed the honour of scoring Town's first ever penalty in a 7-0 victory at Saxmundham.

SATURDAY 23rd DECEMBER 2000

Two goals from Norwegian striker Ole Gunnar Solskjaer sunk 2-0 at Old Trafford in the Premiership. The crowd of 67,597 stands as the biggest ever to watch an Ipswich league game.

FRIDAY 24th DECEMBER 1909

Resilient full-back David Bell was born in Edinburgh. Despite a career interrupted by World War II, Bell amassed 187 Blues appearances and played to the age of 40.

SATURDAY 24th DECEMBER 1949

Scotsman Neil Myles scored twice on his debut in an enthralling 4-4 draw with Crystal Palace in Suffolk. Myles was an influential player at Portman Road, winning two Division Three (South) titles.

SATURDAY 25TH DECEMBER 1937

Left-winger Len Astill notched for the fifth straight game as Town went down 3-2 to Norwich City reserves at a foggy Carrow Road.

WEDNESDAY 25TH DECEMBER 1946

Town's Christmas Day trip to second-place Queens Park Rangers ended with a 3-1 win in front of 15,000 spectators. Tommy Gillespie, Stan Parker and Tommy Parker scored.

THURSDAY 26TH DECEMBER 1963

Town suffered their joint worst defeat as Fulham won 10-1 at Craven Cottage. Graham Leggat scored a hat-trick in three minutes, the fastest ever recorded in First Division history.

THURSDAY 26TH DECEMBER 1968

Rugged centre-half Derek Jefferson became the first player to be sent off at Portman Road for two bookings as Town lost 3-1 to Chelsea.

THURSDAY 26TH DECEMBER 1985

Micky Stockwell made his Blues debut in a 1-0 win at Coventry with Mich D'Avray scoring the winner. Stockwell scored 45 goals in 610 appearances for Town and was renowned for his incredible stamina and energy as well as an ability to play in virtually any position.

MONDAY 26TH DECEMBER 2005

Future Town flop Jon Macken scored and was later sent off for Crystal Palace as they won 2-0 at Portman Road in the Championship.

TUESDAY 27TH DECEMBER 1960

Defender Billy Baxter made his Ipswich debut as the future champions crushed Norwich City 4-1 at a packed Portman Road. Town had won 3-0 at City the day before. Baxter, who was to make 459 appearances and net 22 times, enjoyed plenty of domestic success in Suffolk but was never capped by his country.

SATURDAY 27TH DECEMBER 1975

West Ham United's Keith Robson was sent off as Town won 2-1 at Upton Park over John Lyall's men thanks to Mick Lambert and John Peddelty.

SATURDAY 28TH DECEMBER 1963

Just two days after suffering a record defeat at Fulham, lowly Ipswich gained sweet revenge with a 4-2 pasting of the Cottagers at Portman Road.

WEDNESDAY 28TH DECEMBER 1994

George Burley left Colchester United to return to Ipswich Town as manager. He was unable to ensure Premiership survival in his first season but was to gain success over an eight-year spell.

SATURDAY 29TH DECEMBER 1990

Eight different goalscorers featured as John Lyall's Ipswich and Charlton Athletic shared a 4-4 Division Two draw at Portman Road. The draw meant Town had failed to beat The Addicks in the league despite 22 years of trying.

SATURDAY 29TH DECEMBER 2001

A brilliant 5-0 victory over Sunderland gave Town heart in their attempt to pull clear from the bottom of the Premiership. A wonder goal from Finidi George was the pinnacle of a superb team display.

SATURDAY 30TH DECEMBER 1978

A biggest ever home league win over Chelsea saw Town triumph 5-1 thanks to a brace from Arnold Muhren and goals for Russell Osman, John Wark and Paul Mariner.

SATURDAY 30TH DECEMBER 2006

Jon Macken played his final game in a Town shirt following an unsuccessful loan spell from Crystal Palace in a 2-0 defeat at West Bromwich Albion.

TUESDAY 31ST DECEMBER 1946

Capped 21 times by Northern Ireland, midfield dynamo Bryan Hamilton was born in Belfast. Signed from Linfield, Hamilton left to join Everton for £40,000 after 56 goals in 199 first-team appearances.

SATURDAY 31ST DECEMBER 2005

Luton Town were beaten 1-0 thanks to an excellent goal from Ian Westlake at Portman Road in the Championship. Irish shot-stopper Shane Supple was in fine form to deny the Hatters.

FOOTBALL
On This Day

*History, Facts & Figures
from Every Day of the Year*

ROB BURNETT & JOE MEWIS

£9.99